"Ashley has done it again! This book is filled from beginning to end with powerful truth packed in practical wisdom. In an age of extremism, division, and echo chambers of narcissistic social platforms, this book cuts through the noise, confronts the fear, and takes on the central issues of our time, showing us how to be better humans together. Thank you, Ashley, for being so honest, courageous, and helpful!"

Danielle Strickland, author of *Better Together* and founder of Women Speakers Collective

"Ashley Abercrombie doesn't simply talk the talk. She walks the walk. She is committed to justice because she is committed to God, and that commitment shines through on every page of this book. If your soul is jarred by the not-rightness of this world, and you are searching for the courage to respond without compromising, you will not find a louder cheerleader than Ashley!"

Sharon Hodde Miller, author of *Nice: Why We Love to Be Liked and How God Calls Us to More*

"Ashley Abercrombie is someone I listen to because she is wise and her life backs up her words—which makes her credible in a world and church too often found to be incredible. *Love Is the Resistance* is written in Abercrombie's inimitable way: a colorful, textured, interesting, and wisdom-laden tapestry that demonstrates how to live the reality we Christians proclaim. We can only live that reality of truly loving and forgiving Christians, others, and our enemies if we tell the truth about who we are as individuals and as the church. You'll find humor, joy, wisdom, lament, and straight-talk in these pages. There's no posturing. How refreshing! Take and read."

Marlena Graves, author of *The Way Up Is Down* speaker,

er

"It's safe to say that most o   n
caused by differing opinions   ,

both online and in person. It can be terrifying, ugly, and sad to experience the results that come from clashing with fellow humans these days. It's anything but civil most of the time. Ashley is such a light in this space! She offers perspective shifts that are extremely needed, strategies for loving communication, and so much hope for how things can shift if we come from a place of love. No matter your religious stance or whether you are of faith, you need to read this book."

Allie Casazza, host of *The Purpose Show* podcast and author of *Declutter Like a Mother*

"*Love Is the Resistance* is the kind of sharp, insightful book that will get under your skin and confront your comfort zones. You might get a little defensive—or a lot. Ashley does not hold back in naming conflicts and issues many Christians and churches choose to ignore or minimize. She knows we cannot heal the things we refuse to name. Still, this book doesn't stop at naming; it models a practical way forward. You see, Ashley's discovered what the power of God's love can do, the way it can break every chain and transform us from the inside out. Now she won't settle for anything less—not for you, the church, or the world around us. As we face the challenges of our world today—societies marked by injustice, a deeply divided church, fractured relationships— Ashley offers you an invitation: join the resistance."

Jo Saxton, speaker, leadership coach, and author of *Ready to Rise*

"We find every reason to separate ourselves from others. There is no shortage of disagreement in our digital spaces, dinner tables, and faith communities. In *Love Is the Resistance*, Ashley identifies the reasons we fight and offers practical help to resolve our disagreements while celebrating our differences. You will be blessed by this book!"

Daniel Hill, pastor of River City Community Church and author of *White Awake* and *White Lies*

"I think it's safe to assume that with all our country has been through recently, you have probably had many moments of tension with loved ones, whether face-to-face, on a Zoom call, or in the comments of a Facebook post. With so much disagreement, hatred, and pride pulsing through our country, Ashley Abercrombie's book *Love Is the Resistance* is both timely and necessary for each and every one of us. For the years I've known Ashley, I have deeply respected her passion for Jesus. In this book, she beautifully reminds us how the Bible instructs us to love everyone and gives us practical steps to put into place when division tries to rob us of our love and peace. I can truly say that every person living in our world right now would benefit from reading this book—whether you're struggling to love others or are feeling unloved yourself, Ashley points to the One who can restore you in all of it."

Chris Durso, pastor of Saints Church and author of *The Heist* and *Misfit*

"In the connected age, many of us are malnourished and hungry for whole, reciprocal relationships but struggle to humanize those who do not agree with us. In *Love Is the Resistance*, Ashley Abercrombie gives us a vision of what we, as people of substance and faith, can be and do to build bridges where connection has been lost. With a pastoral and prophetic tone, she welcomes all God's children to see themselves as necessary, valuable, and worthy of connection and love. Love is the way forward, and Abercrombie invites us all on the journey."

Tiffany Bluhm, author of *Prey Tell: Why We Silence Women Who Tell the Truth and How Everyone Can Speak Up*, cohost of the *Why Tho* podcast, and speaker

"Our differences in race, gender, political views, socioeconomic status, religion, and then some sadly continue to divide our communities and even our families. It is refreshing to read a book that is biblically sound and relevant while inspiring us toward solutions that build bridges. Ashley Abercrombie masterfully communicates how leaning into our own humanity and brokenness and that of others with empathy and a desire to seek understanding, whether we agree or not, is an art and skill that must be learned and practiced until it is permanent. *Love Is the Resistance* provokes us to take an honest look into ourselves and take the brave journey of learning to resolve conflict and to disagree without having to cancel relationships. I am thankful for books like this that inspire us toward unity, peace, connection, and learning to love like Jesus loves!"

Irene Rollins, lead pastor of i5 City

"Ashley Abercrombie is a cultural leader worthy of following into battle. In a world where it's so easy to hide, retreat, and build walls to keep others out, Ashley shows us the way through to real connection with her courage, vulnerability, and, most importantly, love for God and God's people. This work isn't for those who long to stay wading in the shallow end of relationship. But with Ashley as a trustworthy guide, should we choose to go deeper, we'll find our way to real and lasting change that lies on the other side."

Ashlee Eiland, formation and preaching pastor at Mars Hill
Bible Church and author of *Human(Kind): How Reclaiming
Human Worth and Embracing Radical Kindness Will Bring
Us Back Together*

"Ashley Abercrombie's *Love Is the Resistance* brings a healing word to a world writhing in the throes of transition. Her prose will make you howl with laughter one minute and weep the next. With the wit of a master storyteller and the care of a pastor, Abercrombie guides readers through a transformational journey they will never forget."

Lisa Sharon Harper, author of *The Very Good Gospel*
and *Fortune: How Race Broke My Family
and the World—And How to Repair It All*

LOVE IS THE RESISTANCE

LOVE

IS THE RESISTANCE

LEARN TO DISAGREE,
RESOLVE THE CONFLICTS
YOU'VE BEEN AVOIDING,
AND CREATE REAL CHANGE

ASHLEY ABERCROMBIE

BakerBooks
a division of Baker Publishing Group
www.BakerBooks.com

Published by Baker Books
a division of Baker Publishing Group
PO Box 6287, Grand Rapids, MI 49516-6287
www.bakerbooks.com

Printed in the United States of America

Library of Congress Cataloging-in-Publication Data
Names: Abercrombie, Ashley, 1981– author.
Title: Love is the resistance : learn to disagree, resolve the conflicts you've been avoiding, and create real change / Ashley Abercrombie.
Description: Grand Rapids, MI : Baker Books, a division of Baker Publishing Group, [2021] | Includes bibliographical references.
Identifiers: LCCN 2021009289 | ISBN 9780801094392 (paperback) | ISBN 9781540901699 (casebound) | ISBN 9781493430222 (ebook)
Subjects: LCSH: Conflict management—Religious aspects—Christianity. | Interpersonal relations—Religious aspects—Christianity. | Love—Religious aspects—Christianity. | Christianity and culture.
Classification: LCC BV4597.53.C58 A24 2021 | DDC 241—dc23
LC record available at https://lccn.loc.gov/2021009289

The author is represented by The Christopher Ferebee Agency, www.christopherferebee.com.

In keeping with biblical principles of creation stewardship, Baker Publishing Group advocates the responsible use of our natural resources. As a member of the Green Press Initiative, our company uses recycled paper when possible. The text paper of this book is composed in part of post-consumer waste.

21 22 23 24 25 26 27   7 6 5 4 3 2 1

To the beloved community of Christ,
full of people I love
and people who drive me to the brink of insanity.
Thank you for making me more like Jesus.

CONTENTS

AN INTRODUCTION NOT TO BE SKIPPED

In a recurring dream, which has been bothering me since 2015, I run down the aisle of a church, a stunning cathedral, slide across the floor on my knees, and tear the burlap sack I'm wearing. My hair looks like it hasn't been washed in six months, wild, burly—I look like a cave woman had a baby with John the Baptist. Then I scream a primal, lengthy, guttural holler that tears through me as I beat my chest, right before I wake up.

I'm not a big dreamer, but every now and then one hits home. Spiritually, I think many of us are this desperate and hungry, returning to our gut instincts. If we're even a little self-aware of the grip pride has on the people of God, we're probably on our knees, begging (maybe even screaming) for change. If you're anything like me, you are sick to death of politics destroying relationships and dividing communities. You might also be tired of the abuses of power across multiple sectors of society, especially in the church. From government to academia to business to clergy leaders, corruption and scandals once hidden are now being revealed. Personally, I'd also like for Christians to actually be Christians.

We've gone through some things the last few years, dear reader. We're reckoning with all the "isms." Racism, sexism, classism, cynicism, everyone-in-the-comments-section-is-annoying-ism. In the public space, Christians are not known for our love, or the fruit of the Holy Spirit, or for uniting together to care for the common good. It's time for change. To put it old school: *repent.*

Repentance presses us to give an honest account of who and where we are. Hope always deals in reality. We cannot cover up all the ugly with useless optimism, nor can we surrender to dystopian terror and hopelessness. The latter tempts me greatly, by the way. I read and watch dystopian fiction like it's my full-time job. But we do not grieve like a people who have no hope. We are able to press in and perceive that God, as per usual, is making something beautiful out of our mess.

My own struggle to live out love in the world we share inspired me to write this book, and my hunch is you might struggle sometimes too.
Love is like oxygen. We need it to live.

I want you to love well. More importantly, I want you to be loved well. To understand that you are worthy of respect, honor, and admiration. To know, without a shadow of a doubt, that your life and your presence matter to God. They matter to others. They matter to us. I want you to deeply internalize your need and desire for relationships. It's okay to need others, to want to give and receive love. But sometimes the humans make this difficult. (Psst! We are the humans.)

14

Have you found it as difficult to engage with others as I have? Has staying true to your convictions while speaking frankly and freely come at a high cost? Do you dread talking to family members and friends because the political divide between you is now unmanageable? Do you struggle to keep your peace, hold your boundaries, and connect meaningfully with others? Are you grieving the loss of your faith community? Have you begun to hate people, communities, and institutions you once loved and respected? Do you feel pummeled by transitions, grief, and the roller coaster of life? Goodness, I'm right there with you, for many of these.

Life shaped us to be who we are. A great amount of the choices we make and the reactions we have to people and circumstances are the result of that shaping. The good news? We can change. We can grow. We can accept our past—the coping mechanisms and learned behaviors—and trust that despite our relational history, we can learn new skills.

You can learn how to communicate and better understand the why behind the conflicts and tensions in your life. You can have difficult conversations, weather the unexpected, and begin to enjoy honest, reciprocal relationships.

I want this book to compel you to lean into love but also equip you to actually do it, so at the end of each chapter, I'm offering you four tools to help you grow: an attitude to adopt, a personal affirmation, a reflection question, and a technique for engaging in conflict and communication with others. I've also included a discussion guide to help you create conversations for change in your book clubs and small groups. (Please message me about your gatherings, so I can pray for you and cheer you on.)

Through my journey in recovery—at the time of this writing, I am seventeen years sober from drugs, bulimia, perfectionism, and dysfunctional relationships—I've learned to manage my triggers, to extend grace, and seek understanding. Why do I do what I do? Why do other people do what they do? This context is critical to connection, relational health, and wholeness. Far from perfection (thank God, because it is a merciless master), I've learned to accept my own brokenness and to be comfortable with others in theirs. In my relationships now there is mutual respect, generosity, and integrity. Still, no matter how far we come in our connections with others, there is no conflict- or pain-free path on this side of heaven. Conflict is normal.

However, resolving conflicts without engaging in screaming matches or manipulative behavior or passively aggressively communicating what we want, think, need, and feel is possible. We struggle to be honest, direct, assertive, kind, and clear. The undertone of so much of our arguing is the fight to be right rather than to connect to a differing viewpoint and see if there is anything to learn. Love is the resistance we need in order to change. Love is wild. It cannot be contained. Radical, unyielding, never-ending, mysterious, and unfailing love. We've tried to control the things of God, the people of God, and God himself for ages. There is a better way.

In these pages, I wanted to be sweet, I really did. I wanted to encourage you how to live and move and breathe in this world, just like Jesus did. I will do my best to do that—but the truth is, I'm not sweet. There's no time for that. The days are urgent, the church in America is a cesspool of sin and hypocrisy, and there is a reckoning running along the same fault line of awakening.

——

There is a deeper movement of the Spirit inside of and around us. Reformation begins from within. Health and holiness in communities begin with each of us collectively deciding to do the beautiful and brutal work of knowing, trusting, and becoming like Jesus. The "isms," culture, media, pulpits, and platforms do not decide who we are and what we become.

I've realized that within the body of Christ are different ideas of who God is, and therefore, what love is. I think we've made little gods that agree with us out of the infinite God of grace. The more we shrink God, the more we shrink love.

Now is the time to do better.

With confidence, I know that I am getting some of this wrong, but to the best of my ability, I'm not going down clinging to my pride, refusing to change, hating the "other." And while I value bridge building, truth telling, and compassionate living, I will no longer cater to Christian communities that value their status and safety, their pride and greed, their rights and politics more than they value Jesus.

We need to honestly own that the American church has lost control of the narrative; our witness is neither wanted nor respected. This ownership is the best thing that could ever happen to us. I learned while at rock bottom in my sorrow and shame that humility is the starting point of a new beginning. Or as Proverbs 9 puts it, "Fear of the LORD is the foundation of wisdom. Knowledge of the Holy One results in good judgment" (v. 10 NLT).

May the worst of our passions and pursuits shrivel up and die so that the God of all creation can resurrect, renew, and restore us into the people and communities we were created to be. My prayer is that we do not miss the opportunity to change, that we will not double down on our intellect, comfort, security, and certainty but rather will mature in the great love and justice of God.

I'm living proof that mistakes, failures, disappointments, and abuses from the past do not have to dictate the future. My community is rich and radical evidence that real love is alive on the earth, that God is good when we are not. Your life is a faithful witness.

Grow in grace, beloved. Repent.

In this with you,

Ashley

Forget the former things;
    do not dwell on the past.
See, I am doing a new thing!
    Now it springs up; do you not perceive it?
I am making a way in the wilderness
    and streams in the wasteland.

Isaiah 43:18–19

CHAPTER 1

Learning Love

Love is resistance. It is a push and a pull, forcing us out of our comfort zones, stretching our borders and beliefs, calling us higher, helping us migrate toward something new. Love is a taste, a melody, a memory. It is a people, a place, a vision, a hope. Love is a fight, a prayer, a counter to cynicism, bitterness, and rejection. It is sorrow and grief, leaving and staying, joy and gentleness, humility and horror.

It is the reason I ache and the reason I live. Words do love no justice. In our desire to discover the reason we are here, to resolve the difficult circumstances and conversations many of us find ourselves in, we must learn to know love. To know what it is and what it isn't. To apply and relieve pressure in order to understand who we are and how our existence alone makes an impact.

Love, like justice, is often theoretical in our minds. It is somewhere out there, otherworldly, idealistic, rather than the quiet, ordinary, daily resolve to love right where we are. Whether we like our life or not. Love is pesky and bothersome because it is not supposed to be irritable and demands that we give up our hurry. Real love deflates our sense of self-importance and presses us to reimagine our time in order to be present and patient. To pay attention. To ask, in the situation I find myself, What is actually happening here? What is required of me? What will produce a great deal of good? Why does this moment feel insignificant and taxing? What (who) am I missing here, in my desire to be somewhere else, in my wishing for something better, something more, in my attempt to control the narrative or the outcome?

Love is a miracle. It is here now. Commanding us to rise from slumber, reviving us to life, testifying to a necessary urgency. *You have one life. It is passing you by. Wake up. Live fully awake and alive.* Do not miss the moment to live, really live, in a time where presence is needed. Patience is lacking, kindness is waning, and we are thirsty for real love. Love that makes us remember who we are, that reminds us we belong to God and to each other.

———

The apostle Paul, a complicated biblical character and a gifted leader in the early church after the death of Christ, wrote letters to pastors and people to encourage them in the faith. His significant offering of instruction, encouragement, and warning to believers about how to live together in the turmoil of the world is still profoundly valuable to us today. His words help us to love well while we're in the process of becoming like Christ.

When I look across the spectrum of newsworthy Christianity, as well as the YouTube sermons, Instagram microblogs, self-described prophets, millions of resources, and perilous comments sections, my heart aches for words of wisdom, for truth that is bound by love. In spite of my gratitude for the easy access we have to clergy leadership, I believe we are longing for a deeper well. People are searching for voices of peace and justice who live with integrity, deal in reality, and instill hope when we are hard-pressed to find it. We need more people who will honestly say these are perilous times, everything is not okay, and while the future is uncertain, we are here together and the merciful Christ is with us.

Paul, often absent in body, remained present to his people through prayer, persecution, and the written word. In one of his letters to Timothy, whom he considered a son in the faith, his words feel like a prophecy fulfilled today.

> But know this, that in the last days perilous times will come: For men will be lovers of themselves, lovers of money, boasters, proud, blasphemers, disobedient to parents, unthankful, unholy, unloving, unforgiving, slanderers, without self-control, brutal, despisers of good, traitors, headstrong, haughty, lovers of pleasure rather than lovers of God, having a form of godliness but denying its power. And from such people turn away! (2 Tim. 3:1–5 NKJV)

Why does this resonate so deeply as *truth*? Worse, why does it seem to accurately describe the very public witness of Christianity in the West? Unloving, unforgiving, slanderers . . . brutal . . . headstrong, haughty, lovers of pleasure rather than lovers of God . . . Good gracious, doesn't that just feel like humanity's baseline?

But why? What leads us toward selfishness? At what point does our generosity and vulnerability, our innocence and laughter, rust into stinginess and impenetrability, offensiveness and cynicism?

Perhaps we lack love. Culturally, it feels like an unbearable emptiness, a desperate need for significance, is perpetually driving us. We feel unable to rid ourselves of loneliness, no matter who surrounds us. Isolation is not reserved for single people or those who live alone. It belongs to those who cannot bond or attach due to past and familial trauma, to those who are perpetually trapped in toxic, dysfunctional relationships, to those whose addictions and anxieties keep them from fully engaging in the healthy practices of love, to those who long for a life other than the one they are living, to those whose majority connection is digital in nature.

Certainly, many people struggle to overcome pain related to love, which hinders us from both giving and receiving. And to be perfectly honest, genuine love is a holy horror show. To lay ourselves bare, to withhold nothing, to stand naked before another and quietly ask, "Do you still love me?" is a wonderful terror indeed. The places we are most resistant to love are the places we are invited to let love teach us, heal us, and help us see.

———

Life is constantly shaping us. We cannot control what we are born into. We do not choose the foundation of love, lack, or hatred we receive. Rarely is our situation all good or all bad but rather a grey matter of peace, pain, joy, dysfunction, connection, and grief. These established rhythms and routines, however chaotic, monotonous, or absent they are, shape our identity and teach us how we are to live with and relate to ourselves, God, and others. Before we are an adult, this is established at home, at school, and in our communities. We learn as we participate in these places with the people we spend the most time with, starting from birth and continuing throughout our lives. To better establish ourselves in relationships, it is imperative for us to understand where we come from so we can better understand where we are.

Think for a second about the best encouragement you ever received. Who offered it? What did it mean to you in the moment? How does it feel now to remember it? Did it shape who you are and your confidence in yourself and your abilities? Encouragement is powerful. My husband, Cody, talks about encouragement as an opportunity to "put courage in." I've found that the places and spaces we're raised, the people who shape our minds and hearts, either encourage or discourage us from becoming our truest selves.

As people, we tend to gravitate toward the bad stuff. It seals itself in our memory like a bad tape we can't cut off. We play it over and over until it melts into the foundation of who we are. While that can be overcome—God wired our brains to change, to regenerate, to renew—we spend too much of our life and our time rehearsing those words and nursing old wounds. This deeply impacts how we connect and relate to each other, and it hinders or helps our ability to love and be loved. Our conflict and communication styles are informed by our upbringing. I love what Mike Foster, author and founder of People of the Second Chance, says: "We learn love from people who do not love us." How true! Our patterns of relating and bonding with others are too often determined by those who love us the least.

Whether we grow up with two parents, a single parent, foster or adoptive parents, stepparents, other family members, or another kind of caretaker, the years we spend preparing to be an adult shape us tremendously. Peggy O'Mara, author of *Natural Family Living*, writes, "The way we talk to our children becomes their inner voice."[1] We internalize the voices we grow up with and carry them with us wherever we go. Absence is also a voice. When children are left to fend for themselves, rarely asked questions, and suffer from little engagement with a parent, as adults they might operate in the world as though they are a burden to others and struggle to share their dreams and desires and to ask for help in their struggles. If abuse is in the home, children may go on to be adults who perpetuate or put up with abuse, or become some of the almost twenty-one million Americans who wrestle with an addiction.[2] Many adults do not have a fallback plan in the form of family. There is no person who can support them emotionally, spiritually, or financially. Even in homes where there is love, hospitality, generosity, and generational wealth/help, children will still experience some form of dysfunction, because no caretaker, parent, or child is perfect. Home is the first place we learn love and where our ability or struggle to be ourselves and trust and connect to others in meaningful, reciprocal ways begins.

Another critical pathway for our wiring around love and care is our education story. On average, children are in school six hours a day, 180 days per year, for thirteen years straight. That does not include after-school programs, sports, or time at the local library, recreation centers, YMCAs, or houses of worship, which can tack on another two to three hours per day. With commute times added in, this means that most children and teens spend their waking hours with other adults and children who will instill values, teach curriculum, and model community care. For many of us, education is a healthy combination of positive and negative experiences; others experience a long string of good or bad, depending on how authority figures established patterns of relating and potentially hierarchies based on intelligence, appearance, or socioeconomic status.

I mention houses of worship because many of us have a faith story. We had a youth group, faith community, Bible study, or other place we began to learn about God. Or perhaps we learned peripherally, if our only encounters were with people who claimed to follow God. We learned who God is, what he approves of, who he loves, and how we're supposed to behave in order to please him or find his favor. For some of us, that meant discovering we are loved by a good God; that we have a Savior who loves us, a Holy Spirit who is our advocate and guide, and a community of people committed to walking alongside us in solidarity. For others, that might have meant learning God is a harsh, unforgiving father who cares more about our behavior than our connection with him, who sets us in community so we can learn the rules of faith—who is in and who is out—and how we can perform for God rather than be loved by him. The way we see God, as well as our worldview, is informed by our experiences with religion as we mature in age and stage.

Inside these spaces—our homes, schools, and religious gatherings—we develop our internal dialogue and establish well-worn patterns of relating to others and staying safe (or at least comfortable in our role, even if not safe) inside relationships. We are shaped by our familial and cultural upbringing, and that is a determining factor in how we see the world, ourselves, and other people as well as how we contribute positively or negatively to society. The internal dialogue we establish as a foundation in our lives dictates our direction. Or, as Alice Walker said,

> Truly the suffering is great, here on earth. We blunder along, shredded by our mistakes, bludgeoned by our faults. Not having a clue where the dark path leads us. But on the whole, we stumble along bravely, don't you think?[3]

Why do we do what we do? What led us to the person we are, and do we like the person we are becoming? We are blundering along, as Alice Walker says, "not having a clue where the dark path leads us." Miraculously, when we fall we get up again, clinging to some thread of grace we've found that makes life worth living. There are times we struggle to face that darkness, when we find it difficult to deal with the conflicts and tensions in our lives. But confrontation is necessary for change. If we are to internalize the best of our upbringing and let go of the worst, we must honestly inspect and confront what, from our past and present, is shaping our responses to people and circumstances.

From the people who loved me, I learned ridiculous generosity—how to keep my hand and heart open, no matter my circumstances. We are a people who turn up with a casserole when there has been a death. We are people who can sit in pain and trauma and offer our presence so others are not alone in their suffering. We are people who shout and cheer and scream for each other, celebrating accomplishments and championing dreams. We are those who give money when we have it to help with adoptions, nonprofits, groceries, therapy appointments. From this love, I learned that I am welcome, that I can bring my whole self to the table, that I am enough, that I am not too much, that my ambition is holy. They taught me to love is to show up, to give myself to service, to push past barriers, to be a safe harbor, and to be inconvenienced.

But if we indeed also learn about love from people who do not love us, then I've also learned other confusing and sometimes similar messages. That love is silent, that love pretends, that love is *always* hard work and personal sacrifice—and because I'd been told to do it so many times, love is sitting still, looking pretty, and shutting up. To be loved, to survive, I found it necessary to contort my painful, confusing emotions into a smile, to twist the truth of my private life into a glowing public review, to ache with longing for space to be myself.

When I moved from my home of origin, I challenged, though did not overcome, the idea that love's most important quality is staying stuck, remaining loyal, keeping quiet, and isolating unattended. The lie that to be at peace is to live in denial was crushing to me, and the more I denied, the more I repeated unhealthy ways of expressing pain. Growing up, and in my young adult years, love felt like constant tension to me. Depending on the person I was with or the place I was in, giving and receiving love felt marked either by fear, anxiety, and control or by a sense of home, connection, and rest.

Did you also receive confusing messages about love? Where did you feel most at home? Who made you feel free to be wholly yourself? Where did you feel unease and find yourself performing for approval? Who made you feel like you had to be perfect in order to be loved? Part of maturing as a person is acknowledging the voices living inside our heads, untangling the web of labels and names we've been given as well as the expectations and roles we've played that are not true to who we are.

———

Learning love means unlearning fear, not so that we will never be afraid—an honest life is terrifying because it is high risk and high yield—but so that we can better understand why we do what we do and make decisions rooted in integrity that build the life we want to live. Not a life riddled with approvals and permissions but a life of freedom and service. Embracing the good and the bad, coming out of denial and accepting reality, and making peace with our past are how we overcome.

Why does Jesus say, "A new command I give you: Love one another. As I have loved you, so you must love one another. By this everyone will know that you are my disciples, if you love one another" (John 13:34–35)? And why is it a command? The Greek word here means an injunction or order, from the root word *entellomai*: to "command, emphasizing the end-objective, i.e., reaching the purpose (consummation, end result) of an order—i.e., as envisioning how or where it ends up."[4]

The prophetic nature of Jesus's words places all the emphasis on his strategic purpose: on the end goal that, by our love, *everyone* will know that we are his disciples *if* we love one another. Jesus's command to love, and during the entirety of his conversation at that Last Supper, which is over five chapters in the book of John, is him engineering for us how and where love ends up.

There was really no reason for the disciples to gather together other than their love for Jesus, aside from a few who were brothers. Isn't this true of us today? But we do not get a seat at the table only with the people we love; we sit at the table with the people God loves.

This is why love is resistance.

It is urgent Christians recapture the essence of this order to reestablish our standing with God and with each other. We are not known for our love. People do not look at our communal witness and see Jesus. For many, their interpretation of God comes from us, the believers who are seated at the table with Jesus.

The late Rachel Held Evans wrote in her book *Searching for Sunday: Loving, Leaving and Finding the Church*, "This is what God's kingdom is like: a bunch of outcasts and oddballs gathered at a table, not because they are rich or worthy or good, but because they are hungry, because they said yes. And there's always room for more."[5] It is time for us to recognize that we are not too good for "those people" because we're all "those people." A bunch of weirdos and ragamuffins. We are not in the Moral Purity Olympics. What is our self-righteous piety and indignation in light of Christ? Nothing special, I assure you. We are here together in our love for Christ, even if nothing else binds us but his blood. And it is time for us to get our act together.

Just like love, communication is a skill we learn. To help us love ourselves and others well at the table with Christ, in the context of our daily lives, we'll end each chapter with four opportunities for personal growth. Take your time here. Reflection and meditation are helpful for healing and connection. I'm offering an attitude to adopt, an affirmation to speak, a question for reflection, and a technique to connect with God or communicate with others (all the others, even the really annoying, "wish you weren't at the table—but Jesus" others).

As much as I love thoughtful cultural insights, unique takes on Scripture, and stories that help us see ourselves and understand people, knowledge does not become wisdom until it is applied. I pray this practice will serve as resistance to the things in culture that hurry us, hurt us, and bully us into unsustainable, unloving lifestyles and patterns of relating. May we grow together from these pages and let the fruit of our labor—love—be evident to all.

ATTITUDE: I am curious about life, about myself, God, and others.

AFFIRMATION: I am able to thoughtfully examine the voices and circumstances that shaped me, and I am courageous enough to ask God to search me, to see if there is any offensive way in me, and to lead me in the path of everlasting life.

REFLECTION: Why do I do what I do?

TECHNIQUE: Create space for critical thinking and reflection. Try setting a timer for ten minutes every day to sit in silence before God, without distraction or any other influence. Is there anything you want to give God? Is there anything he wants to give you?

CHAPTER 2

Cancel Culture

Cancel culture is like civil court.

Saleena Lockett

I t is so odd to watch Christian leaders disagree on the tenets of faith, on what revival is (maybe not a sea of just White people, as one mild example), and on what the church is and should be—and so adamantly. The stream or denomination is neither here nor there, but the arguments and pride driving our public discourse are disorienting. My faith is my lifeline, and I share it regularly, but the church has been a source of embarrassment and shame for me and for many Christians. From sex scandals to performance without substance to the enmeshment of faith with toxic politics, it's difficult to help people connect Christianity with integrity and love.

Rarely do I indulge in media that I know to be inaccurate or harmful, but like a moth to a flame, I recently watched a podcast interview by a famous social media influencer named Candace Owens. She claims to be a political commentator and Christian, garnering followers and supporters and rising through the far-right ranks as a Black woman by supporting Donald Trump, by holding an anti–Black Lives Matter position, and for her leadership within the controversial organizations Turning Point and Prager University. (Not a real university, by the way. Also not accredited, but it is "a place where you are free to learn.") In this interview she'd invited a well-known Democrat, a tenured professor and ardent supporter of Black Lives Matter, to her show, and commended him for saying yes when so many of his colleagues had refused.

Halfway through the interview, I shut my computer off, frustrated with the lack of actual conversation. The Christian host spent most of the time trying to shred every point her guest made, interrupting every time she didn't agree with him, and not listening to a single word he said. I'm sure the sound bites were great for media clips, and she did sound sharp, like a far better debater than he was, and as if she knew what she was talking about. The problem is, she didn't.

Owens cited conservative news media and other influencers who are now political pundits. (Remember when schooling was required in order to do journalism and report facts? Anyone? Bueller?) She'd selected studies that were rooted in confirmation bias and not truth, and she clearly had no desire to change her mind, regardless of the facts or science presented to her. Her opponent, although brilliant, could not match her speed and pacing, and she out-argued him for shame. *He's right on much of this debate*, I thought, *but she* sounds *right*. James 3 immediately came to my mind as I sat with what I'd heard.

> Who is wise and understanding among you? Let them show it by their good life, by deeds done in the humility that comes from wisdom. But if you harbor bitter envy and selfish ambition in your hearts, do not boast about it or deny the truth.

Such "wisdom" does not come down from heaven but is earthly, unspiritual, demonic. For where you have envy and selfish ambition, there you find disorder and every evil practice. But the wisdom that comes from heaven is first of all pure; then peace-loving, considerate, submissive, full of mercy and good fruit, impartial and sincere. Peacemakers who sow in peace reap a harvest of righteousness. (vv. 13–18)

There was no wisdom or understanding in that podcast. Owens showed no humility or willingness to learn, and from my vantage point, selfish ambition seemed to drive her every pounce. The undertone felt like a fight to be right rather than a desire to connect to a differing viewpoint and see if she had anything to learn. While there should be safer spaces for people to debate issues in America today, this conversation was not an example of a healthy, vigorous debate. And from the comments section alone, it seemed clear people were more thrilled over the shredding of her counterpart than they were about gaining insight and understanding into a perspective they vehemently disagreed with. All in all, there appeared to be no takeaways that produced a positive perspective of the other side. This makes for great YouTube videos but not real-life relationships.

═══

As the digital and analog enmesh themselves into our lived reality, we are learning our public discourse and personal communication styles from men and women seeking to grow platforms, gain followers, sell us products, and "drop the mic" (or the hammer, as the old-timers say). The problem with over-identifying with the methods of people whose livelihood—and position of power—depends on our capacity to buy whatever they're selling is that their methods do not work in real life. The ruthless pursuit of being right and destroying adversaries (or praying God will do so) is not making us more like Christ. We do not gain or impart wisdom. We do not take a step forward in more meaningful, reciprocal, generous relationships. We do not show up as ourselves; instead, we mask our vulnerabilities by leading with what we love and what we hate, who we're for and who we're against. In this way, we digress into various stages of toxicity and our connections become about power and control.

I believe this is what James means when he says, "Such 'wisdom' does not come down from heaven but is earthly, unspiritual, demonic. For where you have envy and selfish ambition, there you find disorder and every evil practice" (vv. 15–16).

Across the spectrum of Christianity, disorder and every evil practice exist. Christians are known for what we are against rather than what we are for. We are clanging cymbals devoid of love, incapable of building bridges, more committed to proving our point than we are to offering the world something it can't find on Prager or CNN. Eugene Cho, in his book *Thou Shalt Not Be a Jerk*, in which he exhorts Christians to not be "jerks for Jesus," cited a study by the Barna Group. Barna surveyed young non-Christians in America about the top characteristics of believers and found that the three most formative in the minds of those surveyed were: (1) anti-gay, (2) judgmental, and (3) hypocritical.[1]

Why isn't our wisdom pure? Why isn't it "peace-loving, considerate, submissive, full of mercy and good fruit, impartial and sincere" (v. 18)? Why do we resist peacemaking, or in the words of the Amplified Version, "peace by those who make peace [by actively encouraging goodwill between individuals]"? Why do our ears listen for ways to correct the world rather than love it? Doesn't true transformation begin with love, not punishment or separation or shame?

It feels as though we are riddled with partisanship, opinions, envy, and selfish ambition—and then we slap Jesus's name on it, call it love, and further divide ourselves into our factions and camps, separating ourselves from those who do not share our beliefs. The world is watching, and as I preached in a sermon about the hospitality of believers, corporately we are not known for our warm welcome. How sad. Is there anyone more welcoming than Christ? It's no wonder that the American church is coming apart at the seams, because we are not using the love of God to hold it together. Well, good. This could be the exact dismantling we need to reset and reorder the body of Christ in the way of Jesus. Richelle E. Goodrich, author of *Being Bold: Quotes, Poetry and Motivations for Every Day of the Year*, wrote, "Church was never meant to be a place for gods to gather, but for devils wanting to shed horns for halos."[2]

When the gods gather, ego is at the center. There is a veil—walls and barriers that separate us, a moral competition for who is right and who is better, who is most like God—instead of the truth that all our righteousness is as filthy rags to our holy, perfect, and powerful Father. Throughout biblical history, the prophets were sent to openly identify the sin and hypocrisy of God's people, to shake us from our false ideas about who we really are, and to imagine and declare another reality in the way of communal covenant love. The prophets called attention to economic injustice, religious violence and oppression, elitism, secrecy, pride, and greed. They also devoted themselves to the health and healing of the community at large. When the prophet Jeremiah received his call from God, he said, "Then the Lord reached out his hand and touched my mouth and said to me, 'I have put my words in your mouth. See, today I appoint you over nations and kingdoms to uproot and tear down, to destroy and overthrow, to build and to plant'" (Jer. 1:9–10).

Jeremiah had the worst life, by the way, because when you are called to uproot and tear down, to destroy and overthrow, no one likes you. You are most unwelcome at faith gatherings. But

37

the truth is, there is no planting or building without uprooting, tearing down, destroying, and overthrowing. Any farmer tilling soil knows this. Chip Gaines shows us how this is done every Demo Day. Great leaders within organizations who inherit new teams know that deconstruction comes before reconstruction.

Restoration and redemption start with dismantling faulty belief systems. In order to do that, confession and repentance must be a habitual practice within the community to establish a safe, consistent, and healthy connection. This work leads to a steady flow of loving God and loving neighbor as we love ourselves. If I love God with all my heart, soul, mind, and strength, it becomes easier to love myself and love others. It's not that we'll never hurt people we love, but it becomes harder to *harm* them. You and I will find it more difficult to wound, offend, and take advantage of people we know are made in God's image. This knowledge shores up our care and compassion for others because we know God himself loves them. So, yes, we may uproot and tear down, destroy and overthrow, but if we stop there, our love is harmful, not helpful. A true prophetic calling ends with *to build and to plant*.

———

When Jesus, who is our High Priest, Prophet, and Fulfiller of every prophecy, died on the cross, the earth quaked, hell began to shake, and the temple veil tore from top to bottom. That veil represented the old covenant. It was a beautifully crafted tapestry made by a skilled craftsman, in a special shade of royal purple, that separated God's presence from the people. The Bible tells us that the veil served to protect the priest, who could not stand in full view of God's holiness without dying, and it was a visual and physical reminder to the people of their separation from God.[3] Hence the need to atone for their sins with a priest present; only one day each year could the priest go behind the veil, as God would cover himself with a cloud of glory to allow the priest to enter. People were not allowed to approach the temple, the mercy seat, or the holy of holies except with a sacrifice ready, so in these places of worship there were restrictions on how men, women, and children could worship God.

This is difficult for me to stomach and to reconcile with the God of mercy and grace I love and worship. But as I grow in my faith, I grow in my understanding of the holiness of God and my gratitude for Jesus, who was the final, perfect sacrifice for our sins. As crazy as it sounds to hang my hat on a God who'd kill his only Son, brutally, on a cross so that I could worship freely, without cultural, religious, and traditional boundaries, that is a mystery I trust and believe in. At Jesus's death, the tearing of the veil served to remove the place of the priest and religious leader as the connection point between us and God. This is worth all the worship in the world because human beings are fallible, are imperfect, and tend to confuse our place as a branch with God's place as the vine. He alone is able to welcome us as we are; he alone is able to change us; he alone is able to receive and help us with pure motives and intentions.

Christ himself is our peace. He reconciles and unites us, because he has destroyed our barriers and put to death the hostility between us. In his resurrection and by his Spirit, we are being built together to become a dwelling in which God lives.[4] With the physical and visual barrier of the veil gone, we can approach God anyplace, anytime. Jesus's death and resurrection justify us and make us holy in the presence of God. Not only do we bear his image but his Spirit also, who testifies to us that we are made perfect and are God's children, and who is our guarantee of what is to come, of our eternal inheritance.[5]

The book of Hebrews is about an exchange of grace, explaining how the old covenant is both fulfilled and dissolved in Jesus and detailing the new ways we can relate to God through the sacrifice of his Son and the indwelling of the Holy Spirit. It assures us of the confidence we can have in approaching God and encourages us to gather together with Jesus as our High Priest and Shepherd. Jesus levels the playing field, dismantles the desire within us to dominate and control (which is not a personality type—you can do this passively, manipulatively, or aggressively), and gives each of us roles and gifts within his body, the church, according to his good grace.

> Therefore, brethren, having boldness to enter the Holiest by the blood of Jesus, by a new and living way which He consecrated for us, through the veil, that is, His flesh, and having a High Priest over the house of God, let us draw near with a true heart in full assurance of faith, having our hearts sprinkled from an evil conscience and our bodies washed with pure water. Let us hold fast the confession of our hope without wavering, for He who promised is faithful. And let us consider one another in order to stir up love and good works, not forsaking the assembling of ourselves together, as is the manner of some, but exhorting one another, and so much the more as you see the Day approaching. (Heb. 10:19–25 NKJV)

Christians do still gather, whether it's on Sundays, in house churches, in their communities for dinner and belonging, or for times of worship, grief, and celebration, but the stirring up of love and good works? Exhorting one another with a sense of urgency? I've experienced these in my friendships and faith community, but are they the public witness of the church?

Our collective witness is more like stirring each other up in angst and strife while confusing, judging, and shaming each other to hell with intense urgency. Comments sections are filled with talking points of Christians' favorite pundits; long-time pastors like John MacArthur are telling women like Beth Moore to "go home," whatever that means; Franklin Graham and Jentezen Franklin are demonizing entire groups of people who don't vote like them; and other Christian men like Jerry Falwell Jr. are going down in a blaze of racist, political, sexual glory. The White American church is in such turmoil publicly that people are not even upset. It is a meme; worse, it is common. Folks outside the church not only roll their eyes at this behavior but they *expect* it.

You cannot even imagine the things I thought as I was watching that interview with the Christian podcaster bent on stirring up strife and shame, or when I saw a well-known worship leader's face plastered on political flyers. You do not even want to know how I respond in my head to the things I read on Facebook. Like Anne Lamott said, "I thought such awful thoughts that I cannot even say them out loud because they would make Jesus want to drink gin straight out of the cat dish."[6]

This leads me to cancel culture.

———

If I'm not mistaken, Christians started the practice. When I think of Jen Hatmaker, Lecrae, and Rob Bell—or further back to Aimee Semple McPherson, Ruby Bridges, Martin Luther King Jr., or Delores Huerta—I think of the Christians on TV, in government, or in business canceling whole people groups with their language both currently and historically: "illegals," "socialists," "Marxists," "welfare queens," "Whites only," "trailer trash." The phrase "cancel culture" is rather new, though the practice is anything but, and I contend that now that the power is shifting with the rise of digital media, cancel culture is starting to affect the people who have traditionally had the most power.

While I am aware that a small minority of people will cancel anything or anyone anytime, for the most part cancel culture is morphing into an outcry for folks to do better. From Harvey Weinstein to R. Kelly to Matt Lauer and more, it has proven helpful in forcing the hand of boards, owners, and executives who refuse to hold accountable those who abuse power. People are losing contracts and followers, opportunities and jobs, because of where they press "like" on social media. The result is men especially, though also some women, are being held more accountable for their actions.

There's not too much excitement around this.

Pastors (mostly male) address cancel culture in series or sermons, presenting "honor culture" as an alternative—without describing what it means to biblically ascribe honor between people and God. They usually mean to honor the leader, and they beat us to death with the "man of God who is called" rhetoric rather than take personal responsibility for the lack of accountability within their leadership. Or within the structures that have allowed people in power to do whatever they want, with whoever they want, whenever they want. Podcast hosts will spend an hour-long episode discussing this within networks like Prager, where the culture is defined by the same type of person's (usually White male) ethos.

In general, I don't see cancel culture as a violation of people's personal rights, such as freedom of speech or otherwise. I see it as an opportunity for people without power to speak up and address injustice that would otherwise go undealt with in society. It's why the MeToo, TimesUp, and Black Lives Matter movements have been so incredibly successful. Social media offers people the opportunity to lead, to tell the truth, and to hold people accountable with less fear and intimidation. Cancel culture is the people's way of saying the usual systems for reporting are broken, so we'll go outside the system to report and create a better way. As my dear friend Saleena says, "Cancel culture is like civil court to me."

Plus, who is really getting canceled? Can we talk about that? At the time of this writing, Jerry Falwell Jr.'s contract entitles him to $10.5 million alongside his resignation from Liberty University, paid out over the next two years.[7] Former Fox News and NBC anchor Megyn Kelly, who was fired from NBC for her racist remarks, received $30 million as her payout.[8] Christian comedian John Crist was accused of and then admitted to sexting and sexually harassing women while on tour, and not even a year later he's making a video in a grocery store about canceled products, back from his "time of healing and reflection." He still has a career. No one pulled his books from the shelves. No pastors wrote him an open letter to address his poor behavior and dangerous beliefs. Another example is Nicholas Sandmann, the Covington High School junior who was canceled due to a viral clip of a video at a pro-life rally in Washington, DC, where he appeared to be taunting a Native American elder. In reality, he was engaged in verbal name-calling with some members from extremist group Black Hebrew Israelites, and the elder's singing was an attempt to bring peace between them. Sandmann sued CNN and the *Washington Post* for showing only a portion of the clip. His payout? $275 million from CNN and $250 million from the *Washington Post*, a little more than half a billion dollars.[9]

Does it go too far sometimes? Clearly! Half a billion dollars, methinks, is too far. So yes, cancel culture does get ridiculous sometimes, like when Twitter tried to cancel Goya for the owner's kind remarks to President Trump. And while helpful for accountability, it is not teaching us how to deal with conflict and injustice in real life. Cancel culture isn't fair, and it is like civil court. For most people in power, there are no severe consequences, but we, the people, will put you on notice.

It's also important to note that many people are intimately acquainted with the real-life consequences of getting canceled.

Women's conferences and networks are not out here in the streets debating cancel culture. We know what it feels like already. Getting canceled is something most women are familiar with. Losing opportunities or relationships for speaking up, being silenced and shamed for telling the truth, getting pushed out of communities or families for advocating for others is the realm we live in. Daily. When canceling is done in seclusion, to a female, a person of color, or any person without power, the personal stakes are high, the silencing is real, and the consequences for truth tellers are costly. Power struggles between domestic partners, adults and children, employers and workers, spiritual leaders and congregants can create opportunities for abuse of power, silence, and shame. The person with the least power is pushed out.

This, I think, helps provide a visceral example of why we needed Jesus to tear the veil, why we needed him to lead us personally and communally. We are incapable little gods, full of ourselves, wide-eyed and lustful, seeking to dominate or be dominated, manipulating and controlling one another, and trying to define the larger narrative of who God is and who he loves. I've had enough, and I know I'm not alone in that. It is enough.

With so much pain in this world, when we are sick to death of ourselves, when we are fed up with the injustice and imbalance of power, we come boldly before the throne of grace to a God who sees and a God who knows. A holy God who is not entangled with political or personal agendas and who will make all things new in the end, a God of justice who will hold people accountable when this world will not. A merciful, faithful Christ, our liberator, in whom we find that the chains within our context hold no real or lasting power. A Spirit of Truth, who is our relentless advocate and comfort.

Do not give in to despair, dear one. Take courage in your God who sees and knows. The final say is not in headlines, cancel culture, or personal pain and setbacks. Give your heart to the small things—be consumed with what and who is in your grasp—the sacred ordinary where the goodness of God is evident. All will be made right in the end.

ATTITUDE: My actions have consequences.

AFFIRMATION: Life is not fair, and I will stop pretending that fairness is what I need to be happy. Sometimes, doing the right thing carries grave consequences, such as the loss of relationship, resources, position, and power. Conversely, some people do the wrong thing, and I perceive them to never suffer a single consequence for their actions. God rains on the just and unjust. He is my source of happiness and joy, not circumstances, judgment, news, or media. I am an informed citizen who focuses on what I can control, not on what I cannot.

REFLECTION: Has cancel culture ever been right about a person, place, or thing?

TECHNIQUE: Track your time on social media. Download an app or use the screen time function on your phone to determine how much media is influencing you on a daily basis. Pay attention to the voices that are influencing you, and after one week, reflect for half an hour. Are your digital habits hurting or helping you grow in your mental, emotional, and spiritual health?

CHAPTER 3

Language Matters

Everyone enjoys a fitting reply; it is wonderful to say the right thing at the right time!

Proverbs 15:23 NLT

Is language a form of violence? Should we be allowed to say anything we want, even if it's hate speech? Who determines what is actually hate speech? What do we censor? These questions are important to many people, especially in the context of free speech. Regardless of our personal values, one thing is certain: we are not allowed to say anything we want if we are Christians. The constitution is not our Bible, and Ephesians 4:29 tells us, "Do not let any unwholesome talk come out of your mouths, but only what is helpful for building others up according to their needs, that it may benefit those who listen."

How we choose to use our words matters, and the more we meditate on ideas, criticisms, and gossip, the more likely we are to adopt those ideas and begin to speak those words. What we speak impacts our soul, our atmosphere, and our connections.

In our fast-paced world, we rarely take the time to thoughtfully reflect on our life. Have you tried to sit still and do nothing for five minutes lately? I mean absolutely nothing . . . no Netflix, no reading, no mindless scrolling on social media. Stillness tends to be difficult for most of us, but it is what we need to become more self-aware, to begin to think about what we're thinking about. Our meditation—what fills our mind consistently—is the very thing that forms our belief system. From our belief system we speak. If our core belief says that freedom means we should be able to say anything, no matter who it harms, then freedom of speech is more powerful in our lives than the words of Christ. If we internalize the idea that being right is the primary goal of our religion, then we might use doctrine to shame, correct, and shun other perspectives.

I've heard people speak about having a Christian worldview. This is a powerful ideal. To see Christ in everything, in everyone, offers endless opportunity for transformation and connection. If we approach creation with the same love and mercy as Christ, then would we not approach all of creation full of God's grace and truth? The problem is, What if our truth doesn't agree with God's? What if our idea of grace is full of exceptions and conditions? And what happens when we attempt to legislate truth onto others? What happens when we confuse a lack of boundaries and wisdom with grace?

Does our self-proclaimed "Christian worldview" find us acting like Christ—serving people, loving our enemies, journeying with others in a personal, powerful way—or are we found in an echo chamber shouting at or avoiding anyone who does not agree with us?

The danger in believing we completely understand the desires and will of an infinite God with our finite mind is that we believe we retain the right to say (and perhaps do) whatever we want to someone who does not fall in line with what we believe.

Worse, we remain unaware of how ungodly our words and actions actually are. It's interesting to me that Jesus reserved his harshest rebukes for religious leaders, not for the people who didn't agree with them. This lack of awareness, and the need to be right about God's will, make many Christians tone deaf to the needs and pain of others.

This doesn't just happen in Christianity. In America, there are few issues we tackle head-on in our nation. Check any of our government processes. Listen to media talking heads. Observe organizational leaders in any sector of society. Heck, check out good old-fashioned Facebook. What appears most commonly is unhealthy debate, death by committee, and gossiping about those we don't like or with whom we disagree.

Most of us avoid conflict. (Don't forget that volatility is a form of avoidance as well.) Many of us would rather talk trash and stay in familiar scenarios, even if they are harmful or at minimum unhelpful, than solve problems. In general, we do not like dealing with difficult conversations (and people) we've been avoiding. I know this is a global, human problem, this need to run from tension and conflict, but here's what I want to say clearly:

Language matters.

I think we've used every reason under the sun to justify slander, gossip, and toxic dialogue that hurts us and harms others. We are in denial about the way our words impact people. In my opinion, we are in need of recovery. America needs to turn up at AA every week, or even in some places every day, because she's drunk. Chugging wild Irish rose from the corner store, trying to walk in a straight line, and hurting others like a drunken hooligan. And step one of the program is coming out of denial. Some of us are doing our work, managing our sobriety, staying healthy, building relationships. But for a whole lot of people? Not so much. I'm not saying it's easy to live sober. We are exhausted. Overworked. Stressed about money, relationships, family, the future. The work to stay sane, saved, and present is something else. But if we don't do it, we'll look for unhealthy ways to relieve the pressure or numb the pain before we explode. And listen: it is hard and tiring to live with an addict. To constantly resist codependency, construct good boundaries, and keep the environment safe without flat-out cussing fools out, on the regular? Exhausting.

On the whole, I think the denial of our need for recovery is why the atmosphere in America is painful for many. It is a problem that we the people do not think about what we're thinking about or give stronger consideration to what we speak. It is a problem that we live restless, hurried, and anxious. It is a problem that we are disconnected from the way we think and talk about others. Other human beings, made in the image of God.

Joseph Goebbels, Reich minister of propaganda in Nazi Germany, said, "No one can say your propaganda is too rough, too mean; these are not criteria by which it may be characterized. It ought not be decent nor ought it be gentle or soft or humble; it ought to lead to success."[1]

The language of hate, clothed in plausible deniability, is working, is it not? It's destabilizing us and confirming the biases we hold deep inside as true. News anchors, influencers on social media, pastors, coworkers, friends, and family members put a fresh stamp on thoughts we've already inherited or internalized. *I knew it*, we think. *All Republicans are racist bigots. All Democrats are baby killers. All immigrants want is to steal our jobs. All poor Whites are trailer trash. All Black Lives Matter supporters are Marxists. No politician can ever be trusted. Every church and pastor is corrupt. Everyone in a service role lives to serve me. If they wanted a living wage, or health care, they should just get another job. Their life is messed up because they just need to make better choices.*

This is how propaganda leads to success. And this is how harmful ideas and words become truth to us. Then we repeat that junk everywhere we go—and call it normal. It leaks out at the dinner table, in a small group, at the water cooler at work, during a playdate at the park. What we think about ourselves, others, and the world around us matters. And once we are fully decided on our beliefs, it becomes harder to change our minds. It's like buying a car and suddenly seeing that car everywhere—we just keep confirming what we think, whether it's rooted in facts or not. We deny the truth in favor of something that agrees with us. Words shape our world.

———

Language is a seed that germinates inside the darkness of our hearts and minds. It will bear fruit at some point: rotten, bitter, nourishing, or sweet. Phrases from childhood, the encouragement of friends, the accusations of enemies, the consumption of our entertainment of choice—all of these form neurological pathways that grow deeper, like ruts on a roadway, the more they live in us. These formidable thought patterns can hinder a growth mindset and keep us from learning. Toni Morrison said, "Oppressive language does more than represent violence; it is violence; does more than represent the limits of knowledge; it limits knowledge."[2]

On July 22, 2020, Florida Representative Ted Yoho stood on the House floor to address his colleagues and constituents and offer an explanation for his interaction with New York Representative Alexandria Ocasio-Cortez. "I cannot apologize for my passion or for loving my God, my family, and my country," he said as he closed his brief, bad apology.[3] Having disagreed with Ocasio-Cortez over her policing policies, he'd stood on the steps of our nation's Capitol and told her she was disgusting, crazy, out of her mind, and dangerous. He then reportedly called her a horrible name.

While not even a little surprising to me, having personally experienced violent language on a regular basis throughout the course of my life, I'll tell you one thing: Mr. Yoho had some serious gall to end his time on the floor with that statement. When I read the transcript, I laughed out loud, recognizing the irony of his closing words with his actions that he was not actually apologizing for.

When I was little, "Thou shalt not take the Lord's name in vain," meant that a certain phrase starting with *God* and ending with *it* was the sum total of that commandment. What I've since learned that it means, through proper Bible study, is that followers of God should have integrity. We don't use the name of the Lord to lie, to oppress, or to use others, nor should we ever use God to spiritualize our bad behavior.

What does God have to do with anything? Are powerful men like Representative Yoho incapable of just saying, "You know what, I got so angry, and I said things I regret, and I am so sorry"? When Representative Ocasio-Cortez, also known as AOC, spoke in response to Yoho's behavior and his insincere apology, she said:

These were the words that Representative Yoho levied against a congresswoman. The congresswoman that not only represents New York's 14th Congressional District, but every congresswoman and every woman in this country. Because all of us have had to deal with this in some form, some way, some shape, at some point in our lives. I want to be clear that Representative Yoho's comments were not deeply hurtful or piercing to me, because I have worked a working class job. I have waited tables in restaurants. I have ridden the subway. I have walked the streets in New York City, and this kind of language is not new. I have encountered words uttered by Mr. Yoho and men uttering the same words as Mr. Yoho while I was being harassed in restaurants. I have tossed men out of bars that have used language like Mr. Yoho's and I have encountered this type of harassment riding the subway in New York City.

This is not new, and that is the problem. Mr. Yoho was not alone. He was walking shoulder to shoulder with Representative Roger Williams, and that's when we start to see that this issue is not about one incident. It is cultural. It is a culture of lack of impunity, of accepting of violence and violent language against women, and an entire structure of power that supports that. Because not only have I been spoken to disrespectfully, particularly by members of the Republican Party and elected officials in the Republican Party, not just here, but the President of the United States last year told me to 'go home' to another country, with the implication that I don't even belong in America. The governor of Florida, Governor DeSantis, before I even was sworn in, called me a 'whatever that is.' Dehumanizing language is not new, and what we are seeing is that incidents like these are happening in a pattern. This is a pattern of an attitude towards women and dehumanization of others.[4]

I chose this particular example because of the polarizing nature of those involved—it's an excellent example of what can happen when we place our politics over our humanity and love for neighbor. Due to her politics, race, age, and/or gender, there are people who believe that AOC deserves this treatment, that she asks for it, that she is the name he called her. This is unacceptable. While she and I do not share the same views on everything, I respect her. I honor her. I know what it's like to experience dehumanizing language from men, strangers and personal connections alike.

One day when I was walking down the street near our former home in Manhattan, pushing my two kids in the stroller, a man who was standing with two other men began to make vile, sexual comments about what he wanted to do to me. As Representative Ocasio-Cortez mentioned, this is so regular for women, and I can usually let it go. But I must have been in a mood, because I turned and began to shout at him to shut up. His words were humiliating. I burned with rage and frustration that men do this, that they speak this way to women.

Obviously there is a danger for all women when we address this behavior head-on. Women in positions of leadership and power, particularly when that role belongs historically to men, risk their reputation and character being publicly attacked on cable news media, social media, and in the workplace. Physical and sexual assault are also a real fear for women who speak up or speak out about this behavior. But that day I felt safe on the New York streets because there were so many people around that it would have been hard to assault a woman with two kids under four. I also felt a bit emboldened by my stature. Standing at six foot two, I feel less threatened by small men with big mouths.

So I told him to shut up. Was his response to stop? To apologize? To acknowledge his inappropriate language? Nope, of course not. He said, "Oh real nice. You like talking like that in front of your babies?"

Apparently, it was fine for him to describe what kind of violent sexual acts he wanted to do to me in front of my sons, but it was not fine for me to tell him to shut his foul mouth. And yes, I do want my sons to know that this is unacceptable behavior, and that when it is safe for me to do so, their mother will do no harm but take no mess from anyone. There should be consequences for men when they speak terribly to women, but because society gives them *none*, they keep doing it.

These are not isolated incidents. As AOC clearly stated, there is a culture of "we're fine with this" in the global ethos when it comes to gender. This is perhaps why one in four women will be sexually assaulted or raped during her lifetime. And *that's just reported cases.* I write in my first book, *Rise of the Truth Teller*:

> Violence against women and sexual exploitation do not happen in isolation; they are endorsed and encouraged with community support. A night club that regularly hosts vulnerable, underage, drunk girls; a college dorm full of adults who watch young women coming home wasted, night after night, without taking action; a neighbor who sees something but refuses to get involved in "other people's business"; a family member who suspects a violation but chooses denial, or who hears a victim share but ignores or minimizes their story—these are all complicit.[5]

When we make women objects or subjects, when we broad stroke or sexualize them as curse words, or call them communists or a member of "the squad," or however else we choose to isolate and dehumanize them, it becomes easier and easier to hurt, use, or abuse them and to not care if anyone else does the same. But we are all real people with real feelings, not to mention a God in heaven who cares about us.

Once, I retweeted a clip of Rep. Ocasio-Cortez dancing outside an office. I loved her youthfulness, red lipstick, and the fun she wanted to inject into the Capitol building. Someone took a screenshot of my retweet and sent it to my pastors, sharing their concern that I also held communist, socialist beliefs that (I guess) were going to destroy our community. Not only was it absurd that their personal hatred for AOC and her policies was somehow transferred onto me, but I'm still trying to understand how a person who says they love God, like Rep. Yoho, and who is over forty is still not grown-up enough to talk directly to me.

We do not have to engage with each other this way. Healthy people are mature enough to engage in a conversation. Without gossip, name-calling, or tattle-telling to people we perceive to hold power to bring correction when we will not. (In the final chapters of this book, we'll talk about practical ways to engage others, to fight fair, to hold firm to our convictions without being a jerk, and to stay in relationship with people who do not share our values.)

I remain grateful that something as simple as politics has provided us with a wonderful example of what not to do. I confess there are times when I behave online and in real life in a way that does not honor people. When our belief systems are challenged, we all suffer triggers and setbacks, frustrations and immaturities. Many Christians have so intertwined faith with politics that they feel like one and the same. But they are not. I get that we might disagree on what the DNA of America should be, what should guide our nation, and what laws should be written. I get that our class, race, and gender distinctions can hinder us from understanding another person's lived reality, why they think what they think, why they do what they do.

Still, is it necessary to assign sweeping judgments to one another, devalue our differing perspectives, and talk terribly about each other even if we are well past our high school prime? Besides this, shouldn't bipartisanship be the goal in the American political decision-making processes? And doesn't building bridges across the aisle mean that we must suspend judgment, walk in integrity, and think of the greater good?

Oddly, but not surprisingly, the same person who sent the screenshot to my pastors very highly values personal and political freedom—just not the same freedom for AOC . . . or me, apparently. Without a single conversation with me, this person placed me in the same political category as Rep. Ocasio-Cortez. How did they decide so quickly what I believed? Why did they think that a retweet meant my endorsement of every single thing this public figure says and does?

Do you understand how crazy this stereotyping is?

Did I not also think this person's beliefs were dangerous to our community? Their view on race, resources, and women felt crushing to me; their language on social media was hurtful to people. But was I sending screenshots to anyone to get them in trouble? No, I was not. Do we not live in a world with others who think differently from us? Does the Lord not instruct us to love even our enemies? Is everyone in our faith community supposed to think like we do? Why do Christians insist on being the moral police of the universe? And why do some individuals assume they've cornered the market on truth and know what's best for all of us? Why do some seek to dominate and control others, to legislate and police them according to personal standards rather than the love of Christ?

Truly, I do not care if you are Republican or Democrat, Independent or Green Party. My close friends and family are all over the map. What I do care about is when we allow politics to inform our theology rather than our theology to inform our politics. When we are unable to critique our party, we are in danger. When we form our ideas and beliefs based solely on our own experience and the rhetoric of political figures and pundits, we have lost the plot. When we make a powerful person faultless, we are in trouble. When we think someone deserved to have something terrible happen to them, when we call them names because of our disagreement with and hatred for them, we are contributing to cultural dehumanization. When we refuse to admit we are wrong, to say we are sorry, we are in danger. When we lose our integrity, we lose our public witness. And we need to quit. *Now.*

Like it or not, we will always find people who infuriate us, who are influencing the direction of multiple sectors of society. Regardless of our political affiliation, we must press in, and we need to listen when something true is spoken that can help us realize our mistakes and help us grow. AOC's words rang true with women across the world, because we know the pain of verbal assault and the pain of an attempted or successful cover-up, intimately. We know when someone apologizes because they have something to lose instead of apologizing because they were wrong. It is easy to see when someone has no intention of changing.

Perhaps this particular moment rang true for so many because people are so tired of God's name being used to excuse bad behavior. And Alexandria Ocasio-Cortez, beloved of Christ, gave a most fitting reply to her colleague.

> I do not need Representative Yoho to apologize to me. Clearly he does not want to. Clearly when given the opportunity he will not and I will not stay up late at night waiting for an apology from a man who has no remorse over calling women and using abusive language towards women, but what I do have issue with is using women, our wives and daughters, as shields and excuses for poor behavior. Mr. Yoho mentioned that he has a wife and two daughters. I am two years younger than Mr. Yoho's youngest daughter. I am someone's daughter too. . . .
>
> In using that language in front of the press, he gave permission to use that language against his wife, his daughters, women in his community, and I am here to stand up to say that is not acceptable. I do not care what your views are. It does not matter how much I disagree or how much it incenses me or how much I feel that people are dehumanizing others. I will not do that myself. I will not allow people to change and create hatred in our hearts.
>
> And so what I believe is that having a daughter does not make a man decent. Having a wife does not make a decent man.

Treating people with dignity and respect makes a decent man, and when a decent man messes up as we all are bound to do, he tries his best and does apologize. Not to save face, not to win a vote, he apologizes genuinely to repair and acknowledge the harm done so that we can all move on.[6]

AOC may not be your cup of tea, but here's the takeaway: when we commit to a shining public display of righteousness without a private walk of integrity, we are like "whitewashed tombs, which look beautiful on the outside but on the inside are full of the bones of the dead and everything unclean. In the same way, on the outside you appear to people as righteous, but on the inside you are full of hypocrisy and wickedness" (Matt. 23:27–28).

We cannot live in denial about who we are, what we think, and what we believe, nor can we allow dehumanizing language to hinder us from learning. Language matters. Christians are commanded to watch our words. We are also commanded to love all people, not just the people who agree with us. May we call each other higher, and may humility and true repentance be our portion.

ATTITUDE: I learn from people I disagree with because they are human beings made in God's image. He loves them, and I will not demonize or despise a person God created and loves.

AFFIRMATION: My heart is built to withstand pressure, and to honor God, myself, and others. Yielding to constant criticism, cynicism, and bitterness is not who I am. I am a person created in the image of God, able to love and respect others. Even when I disagree, I will choose to honor with my thoughts, words, and deeds.

REFLECTION: Jesus, you are a non-anxious presence to me. Your lovingkindness is unhurried and of great comfort. Help me to experience you as you really are and not as I push you to be. Help me to slow down, think critically, and be a comforting, gentle presence to all who encounter me.

TECHNIQUE: Set a timer for ten minutes. Close your eyes and picture a person whose beliefs and ideology you despise. Perhaps it is a family member, former friend, fellow church member, preacher, or politician. Notice the tension in your body—where is it? Notice any anxious or angry thoughts and feelings. What phrases are coming to mind? Where is Jesus as you think about this person? What is his posture toward you (Matt. 11:29)? Can you feel his tenderness and love for you? Can you imagine Jesus with the person whose beliefs you despise? Allow yourself to picture his lovingkindness toward that person. God does not ask us to like everyone but he does ask us to live at peace with everyone. What will it take for you to cultivate peace in your heart toward them?

CHAPTER 4

Love Thy Neighbor

The body of Christ is in process. Some call this a revival or a reformation. I like to call it a rebuke. Early on in my ministry journey, an older woman sat me down to tell me the four tenets of a sermon that will actually serve people: exhort and reprove, encourage and rebuke. "You can't give them all fluff, and they don't need you to constantly tell them what to do. Care for them. Point them to Jesus," she said. When I think about her life, the way she gave herself to showing me how to pray and hear from God and how to love broken people, I feel profound gratitude. She was an overflowing well of wisdom for me as a wayward believer in Christ. She spoke her mind but was as patient as the day is long. As I began to waddle in the way of Christ, her solidarity helped me grow exponentially. The encouragement she gave was always specific, and she maintained an unshakable belief in my potential to grow into the image of Christ. Because of her love, when she rebuked me, I took it like a champ because I knew it would help me grow. Hebrews 12:5–6 says, "My son, do not make light of the Lord's discipline, and do not lose heart when he rebukes you, because the Lord disciplines the one he loves, and he chastens everyone he accepts as his son."

Rebuke means to reprimand or censure. To strongly warn or restrain. A fabulous meme recently made its way around the socials. It said, "At this point, Jesus doesn't need to take the wheel. He needs to pull over and whip some of y'all with his flip-flop." I feel this deep in my bones. The evangelical church is out of control. A reprimand is needed.

In January 2021, Trump supporters who were unable to accept the election results of President-Elect Joe Biden and Vice President–Elect Kamala Harris arranged a rally on Capitol Hill.[1] The rally escalated quickly into what some called a violent riot and others a failed insurrection on the Capitol by a mob that included White supremacists, members of conspiracy groups such as QAnon, and ordinary people who felt entitled to revolt—apparently no matter who they hurt or what they destroyed. For the first time, a Confederate flag was marched through the halls of Congress, while members of the House and Senate were quickly ushered into hiding places until Capitol police cleared the area. Images of the day show us a noose constructed outside the building and men dressed in military gear storming the Senate chamber with zip ties, prepared to commit God knows what potential crimes.

How does this tie in to rebuking the body of Christ? First, let me say my anger at some famous pastors and clergy leaders runs on the border of bitterness. Their vigor for Donald Trump as God's chosen man, without critique, and their selfish allegiance to nationalism and fame make them complicit to the actions of January 6. This is not an issue of Republican or Democrat, or whether or not people of faith should engage in politics. The right to vote for the party we choose is democracy, and I thank God for it. It is the toxic enmeshment of faith and politics that frustrates me, and it has led to unhealthy discipleship that has unleashed something dangerous in our nation.

The most devastating picture I saw from this terrible day in America was a visual captured on the news. Just above the storyline banner that ran across the lower third of my screen that said, "Insurrection on the Capitol" was a sign in the crowd that said "Jesus Saves." I wanted to shout at the TV! Why do you need a "Jesus Saves" sign at a political rally, number one; and number two, why are people so unafraid to take the Lord's name in vain? *This is not God*, I kept repeating. *This is not Jesus.* For years, I've watched the public witness of the church go up in flames. And you know what—let it burn. This is not a witness. This is idolatry. Rebuke us, Lord. Censure us. Make us new.

Ezekiel 34 burns in my heart for the body of Christ. Over the years, when I've experienced offense or hurt from a person in church leadership, I go to this passage. It reminds me what a good shepherd is and is not. I feel tender toward our fallible nature as people and pastors when I read it, and while it reconnects me to Jesus, the Good Shepherd, the one who is always loving, tender, and true, I am greatly comforted by God's way of rebuking corruption in leadership.

What I had not paid enough attention to is the next part in the chapter, where God deals with the flock, the community of believers.

Ezekiel 34:17–24 says:

And as for you, my flock, this is what the Sovereign LORD says to his people: I will judge between one animal of the flock and another, separating the sheep from the goats. Isn't it enough for you to keep the best of the pastures for yourselves? Must you also trample down the rest? Isn't it enough for you to drink clear water for yourselves? Must you also muddy the rest with your feet? Why must my flock eat what you have trampled down and drink water you have fouled?

Therefore, this is what the Sovereign LORD says: I will surely judge between the fat sheep and the scrawny sheep. For you fat sheep pushed and butted and crowded my sick and hungry flock until you scattered them to distant lands. So I will rescue my flock, and they will no longer be abused. I will judge between one animal of the flock and another. And I will set over them one shepherd, my servant David. He will feed them and be a shepherd to them. And I, the LORD, will be their God, and my servant David will be a prince among my people. I, the LORD, have spoken! (NLT)

Are you catching this? God is upset with the folks in the body who are content to keep the best of the pasture for themselves, content to drink clear water and muddy the rest for the other people. In their selfishness, in feeding and tending and serving themselves, the "fat sheep" in the community neglected to recognize that their consumption came at a cost to the rest of the flock. Their satisfaction meant hunger, thirst, sickness, abuse, and a scattering to the margins. From this passage, we can deduce biblically that God wants us to consider the lived experience of the entire body, not just our happy little pasture.

The whole body of Christ is not having your exact experience. To ask pointedly, Is your gospel good for people who do not live like you or look like you? Is it good for those who don't believe what you believe? Is it good news for the poor and marginalized? Is it good news for the rich and powerful? Is it good news for those outside your nationality, ethnicity, and gender? Is the way you get and use your resources good news for your community? Because if it is not, it is not the good news of Jesus Christ. Sometimes we fight for our rights and our way at the expense of biblical commands; therefore, we are also fighting for ourselves to have the best at the expense of others.

Are you alone in your context and way of living? No. But are you to consider what others are going through and make a change if necessary? Yes. Because God comes to separate the sheep from the goats, and he feeds, heals, and tends to the scrawny sheep, and he brings correction to the fat sheep. He gathers us together, and he heals us. Some of us he heals by emptying, and some by filling. Probably, we'll experience both, but Ezekiel 34 teaches us that some of the flock are consistently at an unbearable disadvantage.

———

Selfishness kills connection. So does cluelessness. Determined ignorance. I sometimes wonder if that's why the expert in the law in Luke 10 sought to justify himself, asking, "Who is my neighbor?" He's not so different from us. Prior to this question, the Pharisees debated Jesus about resurrection, taxes, offerings, and poor leadership. It's interesting to note that they were usually debating about theology and justice but rarely practicing either. None of us like to read biblical texts and admit we look more like the Pharisees than like Jesus, but it is true that we love to fight over who is doing justice the right way, who is leading the best and the worst, and which politics are the right ones according to God.

While we try to show off our intellect, rank people and movements by what we think is right, and avoid doing the work by constantly critiquing it, the world is not only moving on without us (because justice waits for no one) but people suffer. The witness of the church suffers. This is similar to the text in Ezekiel 34 because it's easy for believers, especially in America, to cultivate a happy little pasture where we feel secure, safe, and comfortable. It's easy to forget that downstream from our decisions are hurting people receiving what we've trampled down and muddied.

So, how does the good Lord respond to the question, Who is my neighbor? He tells the expert a story about a Samaritan, one who was likely on the scattered-from-the-flock side of the equation, and the person who this man likely felt the most animosity toward. Without judging their reasons for not stopping (maybe they were good ones, who knows?), Jesus points out that the priest and the Levite didn't stop to feed, to tend, to help the man in the ditch, but the Samaritan did. What a powerful critique for the Lord to essentially communicate: the one you hate, the heretic, the one whom you suspect can do no good is the most merciful and the one we call good. Jesus then asks Smarty-Pants Religious Man, Which of the three was a neighbor to the man in the ditch?

"The one who had mercy on him," he responds. To which Jesus says, "Go and do likewise" (v. 37).

I'm suggesting that we take Jesus's words seriously and get busy being merciful on this side of heaven, that we recognize there's a give and take in community. If we are fat and happy, leisurely and intellectually debating with God, "Who is my neighbor?" while people are dying in ditches, hungry, thirsty, abused, in despair, and separated from us, then what is our Christianity? Further, perhaps our judgments and assumptions are keeping us from seeing people through the lens of mercy, from loving people like Christ. Worse, they are hindering the church from doing justice. Blinded by our privilege and our intellect, we assume we are better than we are. What we know about God has not yet translated into how we demonstrate the love and power of God; in reality, we are sometimes far worse than those we presume are the most reprehensible in society. Yes, if our talk doesn't match our walk, then we should probably not assume we are better than those heretics. Which was Christ Jesus's point in this parable.

Last I checked, all our righteousness is filthy rags to a holy God,[2] so it's time to stop pretending we are more righteous or holy than anybody else. Don't believe your own hype. Every thought you think is not the truth, so don't internalize lies about yourself or others. You are beautiful, powerful, and worthy of love and respect. You are also not the most important person on earth. The world does not revolve around you. Center yourself in Christ and humility will lead you. It is time for us to surrender our need to be right. To resist the notion that our individual decisions do not affect the community at large. To recognize that the Lord will separate the sheep from the goats. Matthew 25:31–32 says, "When the Son of Man comes in his glory, and all the angels with him, he will sit on his glorious throne. All the nations will be gathered before him, and he will separate the people one from another as a shepherd separates the sheep from the goats."

With all the scandals in the church, the corrupt leadership, and the hurt that remains in members and former members, it's easy to assume that only leaders will be held accountable by God for the impact of their attitudes and decisions on people. We can try to shift all blame for the state of the church onto the clergy, but the truth is, the whole body will be held accountable. I am responsible. You are responsible. We are responsible for the state of the body of Christ. If we are going to move forward, then we must receive this rebuke from the Lord. Now is the time to repent and remember that there are no conditions on loving our neighbor.

Carlos Rodriguez, founder of Happy Givers, has made my favorite sweatshirt, which says:

Love Thy Neighbor
Thy Immigrant Neighbor
Thy Black Neighbor
Thy Atheist Neighbor

Thy Muslim Neighbor
Thy Depressed Neighbor
Thy Conservative Neighbor
Thy LGBTQIA Neighbor
Thy Disabled Neighbor
Thy Indigenous Neighbor
Thy Jewish Neighbor
Thy Progressive Neighbor
Thy Incarcerated Neighbor
Thy Homeless Neighbor
Thy Latinx Neighbor
Thy Addicted Neighbor
Thy Millennial Neighbor
Thy _____ Neighbor[3]

Again, there are no conditions on loving our neighbor. We don't get to opt out of love because it feels hard. Matthew 5:43–48 says,

> You have heard that it was said, "Love your neighbor and hate your enemy." But I tell you, love your enemies and pray for those who persecute you, that you may be children of your Father in heaven. He causes his sun to rise on the evil and the good, and sends rain on the righteous and the unrighteous. If you love those who love you, what reward will you get? Are not even the tax collectors doing that? And if you greet only your own people, what are you doing more than others? Do not even pagans do that? Be perfect, therefore, as your heavenly Father is perfect.

The gospel of Jesus Christ is a tough pill to swallow, but it goes down good with grace.

ATTITUDE: Generosity—open hands, big heart.

AFFIRMATION: I am hidden with Christ in God (Col. 3:3). He is able to help me love the neighbors I like and the neighbors I don't. His grace enables me to do what I cannot do on my own. I choose to extend that grace to others. I will not opt out of love.

REFLECTION: When I look at the "Love Thy _____" list, I struggle the most with _____. Why is this true? Holy Spirit, help me to see how my upbringing, news cycles, and other people's opinions have formed my ideas of love more than you have.

TECHNIQUE: Know thyself. If we are unaware of how our past is impacting our present, we will struggle to understand why certain situations or people set us off. We'll also struggle to understand why our connections cannot be strengthened, even when there is a possibility for friendship or deeper relationship. Think about your life, where you come from, what makes you feel out of place, and who feels like they are always putting you in your place (even if they are not). How can you overcome the hurdle of your past experiences that might be impacting your present relationships?

CHAPTER 5

Love Is the Resistance

What is love, really; how did we learn it, and what has it taught us? That we need to be nice? To be right? To be perfect? To lie? To hide? To manipulate? To control? To be quiet? To submit? To stand down? To stand up? To hate? To help? How is love living in and through us, and what does that mean for the connections we peripherally and personally share?

Through helping you reflect on the ways you are shaped to think, to live, and to be in the world, I hope to offer you solutions to the conflicts in your life. Through helping you identify your expectations of yourself and others, as well as how you handle obstacles and arguments, I hope to help you live beyond perpetual disappointment and the consistent discouragement that you cannot engage in and resolve conflict. Conflict is not only a normal part of life but can be handled with candor and kindness, and you can release yourself from controlling outcomes and narratives in order to feel satisfied. Communication is a learned skill, which means you can grow in it and begin to approach disagreements and tension from a place of health rather than a place of fear.

But how are we supposed to do that in a world that so easily divides us? That can feel so volatile and vicious?

As I write this, today is the first day in my last pregnancy that I've had no pain and no sickness. My husband is sleeping late, which he hasn't done since the middle of March 2020 when, without warning, I couldn't get out of bed for two days. We thought I might have contracted coronavirus during our recent cross-country road trip; instead, my breasts began to ache and, well, I knew. I was pregnant.

The theme song of the kids' YouTube show *Blippi* is the soundtrack to this writing. My boys interrupt every eight to ten minutes to ask me for more water, for a blanket, or to wipe up milk from the table. Heaven only knows where their neat freak streak comes from, or why they insist on clean space at the ages of five and three. Not that they'd think twice about pouring out a bucket of LEGOs in their room, making a death trap for our entire household.

Mama was one of their first words. *Mama.*

Shrieking with joy and repeating the syllables just so those squishy babies with long lashes would say it again, I'd snuggle and encourage them to say it some more, my heart filling with laughter.

Mama.

It's the same thing George Floyd said in the final moments of his life. Could he see her? Was he so close to heaven, as he lay almost dead in the street, that he could see his mother? Were her arms open to him? Did she kneel by his side as he crossed over? Was her heart filling with joy to hold him again, aching with sorrow to see his life reduced down to nine minutes with a White supremacist's knee on his neck?

═══

Supremacy is the tea I'm steeped in.

Born into a world built for me but also built to control me, I implicitly learned outside the home that I was superior. I was supposed to be the best, the prettiest, the smartest, the most genteel, the classiest, the one with the answers. How can a person be all these things? Especially when the contrary messaging at home to all the women was, "You ain't nothin', probably ain't gon' be nothin', so sit down and shut up. Don't get above your raisin', little girl. You ain't better than nobody. Now fix all this. Clean up my mess, and don't you tell a soul about it neither."

My parents were from poor White families in rural counties. Only one of my four grandparents finished high school. My grandfather, the smartest man I knew when I was growing up, could not read or write. My mom busted her butt to lift us from minimum wage mill workers to a working-class family through her decision to become a registered nurse, the first in the entire family, on both sides, to ever get a degree.

But we inherited a mentality about people who thought they were better than us, mainly rich and powerful people. We were raised at bare minimum to be suspicious of them, and at worst to hate them, but also to please them, to try to be like them, so they'd know we were just as good as them, if not better. Everything in my formative years seemed to feed my sense that I was never enough, that I was inferior and superior at the same time. From my looks to my busted car to my knockoffs from Value City, I created an image that said "I belong here," but also "Screw you."

I took pride in my connections to others, my understanding of what it meant to be from the wrong side of the tracks, the compassion I inherited from my parents, and the way no one in my circle looked the same. I now know that I saw myself as morally superior to rich people who, I believed, could never understand the grief and anxiety of never having enough, never being enough.

It's an interesting thing to be steeped in supremacy but riddled with powerlessness, especially in a social order that demands perfection. How can you be superior and inferior at the same time? Is this the conundrum with privilege? Will this remain the conflict within me? I never have to worry that the cops will kill me, that I won't be able to get a job, that I'll ever be deported or arrested or discarded because of the color of my skin or the ableness of my body—but I'm still a woman.

I know how to lie still during a rape, to lift myself high above my body in order to survive. I've felt the sting of a man's hand on my face and cowered beneath the words of too many people who threatened my reputation, my job, my relationships. For the longest time, my strongest associations were not where I was superior to others but where I was inferior to them, and if I wasn't perfect, I had to pretend I was.

All these things divide us. Race. Money. Gender. Our opinions about them. It doesn't have to be this way, but so often it is. I think of Gina Crosley-Corcoran, who wrote the article "Explaining White Privilege to a Broke White Person." She writes:

> I, maybe more than most people, can completely understand why broke white folks get pissed when the word "privilege" is thrown around. As a child I was constantly discriminated against because of my poverty, and those wounds still run very deep. But luckily my college education introduced me to a more nuanced concept of privilege: the term "intersectionality." The concept of intersectionality recognizes that people can be privileged in some ways and definitely not privileged in others. There are many different types of privilege, not just skin-color privilege, that impact the way people can move through the world or are discriminated against. These are all things you are born

into, not things you earned, that afford you opportunities that others may not have. For example: Citizenship, Class, Sexual Orientation, Sex, Ability, Gender Identity.

As you can see, belonging to one or more category of privilege, especially being a straight, white, middle-class, able-bodied male, can be like winning a lottery you didn't even know you were playing. But this is not to imply that any form of privilege is exactly the same as another, or that people lacking in one area of privilege understand what it's like to be lacking in other areas. Race discrimination is not equal to sex discrimination and so forth.[1]

There's much discussion around privilege but little understanding, especially within communities who have the most access to resources and security. People tend to hunker down into self-protection mode, guarding what they own, what they've worked for, and the relationships and achievements they feel provide a sense of significance, often at the expense of others with fewer opportunities and means. And the gap between our lived realities grows.

In 2020, in the middle of the COVID-19 global pandemic, many people were far removed from their daily and weekly echo chambers save the digital ones, with perhaps more time to thoughtfully reflect and consider themselves and their values. That summer, we were thrust in the middle of a global protest against another pandemic, one of racism and White supremacy, with the murders of Ahmaud Arbery, Breonna Taylor, and George Floyd opening the floodgates of truth and boldness.

Many people wondered, Are we at a tipping point?

There were protests in all fifty states in America, along with eighteen other countries on our behalf. During one of the rallies that summer, I stood on a corner in one of the Whitest neighborhoods in the valley of Los Angeles with a sign that said: "Mamas for Black Lives—George summoned us all." My dear friend Lynette, part of a mommy group, had organized a hundred people or so to stand against the injustice of racism and White supremacy. In this group, mamas are teaching and learning nonperformative allyship to families and seeking to raise anti-racist children. This level of national and global engagement is unusual, to say the least; so are White suburban mamas marching in the streets, encouraging each other to be and raise anti-racists.

That summer it seemed people who were generally removed from the racial justice conversation began to speak out. Respected leaders began to turn from their positions of support for the Trump administration. General "Mad Dog" Mattis released a statement to the *Atlantic* denouncing President Trump. Following this, the governor of Alaska publicly stated that she was unsure if she could support Trump in the 2020 election. (This from the home state of Sarah Palin, whom the excellent PBS documentary *America's Great Divide: From Obama to Trump* determined to have originated the fake news movement.) The television evangelist Pat Robertson, known for his conservative stances, publicly rebuked the president first for his response to the nationwide protests and later for his rejection of the 2020 election of Joe Biden. Houston megachurch pastor Joel Osteen marched alongside George Floyd's family in a Black Lives Matter protest.

The body of Christ continued to divide, and many remained surprised to see support from formerly silent leaders in government and the church. Did that mean pigs were flying? Or that the sound of Revelation trumpets would be heard soon? Would the feet of Jesus soon land on the ground of Armageddon? Or was White America finally, maybe a little miserably, waking up?

Thankfully, many well-known Christian clergy leaders have renounced racism for the first time. Some have hosted interviews with Black therapists, pastors, and activists to publicly unpack the history of White supremacy and racism in America. People in their congregations and other followers of their large platforms heard about its significant impact on Black Americans. White Americans courageous enough to remain in congregations and online communities have had a fresh opportunity to see that White supremacy is not just a hooded character in the KKK or a neo-Nazi in the alt-right but lives in the air we all breathe.

I'm grateful to have witnessed Christians in my life who'd gossiped about me in the past, told me I have a political spirit, or told me to leave social justice out of the church—even those who formerly believed peaceful protests were an act of rebellion—protesting in cities across America while holding Black Lives Matter signs. From the NFL to Tiffany's to Chick-fil-A, many organizations have publicly released social media posts, emails, and statements about racial injustice in America. While there is still great critique over the timing, and activists question the integrity in their words, it is clear that many people who were formerly silent, or who even opposed racial justice movements, have realized that a line in the sand needed to be drawn.

On the other side of that line are plenty of evangelical leaders, right-wing commentators, and other people across the nation who've doubled down on defining the right way to protest, blaming Antifa agitators, destroying George Floyd's and Breonna Taylor's character, and discrediting any good of the Black Lives Matter movement. As the protests multiplied, so did conspiracy theories about a global cabal, the Chinese Communist Party, and Trump as savior for America. The problem with such theories is that they are a moving goal post. There's always a new truth to chase, a new prophecy to believe in, after the last one did not come true.

And so, the polarization grew. Online and in real life, we now knew where people we love stood. Even those without a dog in the fight or who landed less on any extreme end of the spectrum could now feel unsure how to relate to family members, colleagues, and fellow/former church members.

How on earth do any of us move forward, as we stare across that line in the sand?

———

I wonder, in considering all of this, where you see yourself. Are you in a standoff with the "other side"? Trapped in the middle? Or standing firmly in your conviction to tell the truth and love like Jesus? Who do you harshly judge? I also wonder, Do you and I leave room for people to not be who we expected them to be? Does a social media post, a hard conversation at the dinner table, or a strong stance on an issue equal the sum total of who a person is? (Maybe. Especially if they are racist, sexist, or bitter and angry trolls. Let them go on and work through that without you, if it's possible. Of course, this is a whole other story if you're, you know, married to them. We'll cover that in chapter 9, fam.)

Do we allow people to evolve, or must they remain in the box we've placed them in? And what does that say about our connections to others? Do we need them to stay where they are to feel good about where we are? Are we tethered to our judgments, or do we let people change for the better? Finally, who has cornered the market on truth? Do we think we are right about everything we think, or is there room to be wrong? Because sometimes we are.

Still, thought leaders across every sector lock heads over everything but seemingly refuse to consider, or care for, all the human collateral damage caused by their privileged, intellectual arguing. So many of those big ideas, on either side, trickle down into the comments sections, dinner tables, and psyches of those of us who consume them consistently. Then, it can feel like we are shouting, as we attempt to pressure everyone toward our perspective but remain unable to chart a firm way forward.

We are butting heads about the bias of our news sources, the trustworthiness of the government, our silence on racism or our desire to be anti-racist, and the believability of the conspiracy theories—and we are neglecting the most important matter at hand: justice. Which is not a curse word or cultural trend. Justice is the heart of God.

Micah 6:8 says, "He has shown you, O mortal, what is good. And what does the LORD require of you? To act justly and to love mercy and to walk humbly with your God." Matthew 23:23–24 gives us a staunch and sober warning:

> Woe to you, teachers of the law and Pharisees, you hypocrites! You give a tenth of your spices—mint, dill and cumin. But you have neglected the more important matters of the law—justice, mercy and faithfulness. You should have practiced the latter, without neglecting the former. You blind guides! You strain out a gnat but swallow a camel.

Are we so stubborn and small-minded that we'd rather die on a political hill than live a life of justice, mercy, and faithfulness? Must we so desperately need to be right that we'd strain out a gnat and swallow a whole damned camel?

Amos 5:22–24 in *The Message* paraphrase of the Bible makes it plain:

> I can't stand your religious meetings. I'm fed up with your conferences and conventions. I want nothing to do with your religion projects, your pretentious slogans and goals. I'm sick of your fund-raising schemes, your public relations and image

making. I've had all I can take of your noisy ego-music. When was the last time you sang to me? Do you know what I want? I want justice—oceans of it. I want fairness—rivers of it. That's what I want. That's all I want.

Like Amos, speaking on behalf of God, I am fed up. Enough is enough. We are missing the mountain for the molehill. Whether we know it or not—and I intend to persuade you toward this—we are remarkably connected to each other and must develop an unreasonable love and high regard for human life outside our own personal experience, beyond our "camp."

It is my belief that beneath our veneer lives a visceral pride that hinders us from civil discourse, and this pride is hurting our relationships. Our (maybe fanatical) determination to spend our meditative energy on the thoughts, declarations, and opinions of news anchors, presidents, politicians, YouTube stars, professors, clergy leaders, and social media posts is leading us toward isolation, anxiety, and fear and away from the love of God and the way of Jesus. Dan White Jr., author of *Love Over Fear: Facing Monsters, Befriending Enemies, and Healing our Polarized World*, shared this on Twitter: "The power of polarization is that it can take people that have something in common, emphasize their differences, harden their differences into disgust, and then turn disgust into blatant hatred for one another."[2]

I see this in us; do you? The connections between us are causing conflict.

Without thoughtful reflection and personal examination that includes a clear inventory able to help us honestly admit who we are and locate where we are, we will be unable to press into a more merciful, meaningful life of love and genuine relationship. Without understanding what our connections are, we lack the critical capacity to think for ourselves or make decisions that honor our own integrity and the dignity in other people who encounter us. I believe we can do better than arguing at our dinner tables, sweeping issues under the rug, bickering and villainizing in our houses of worship, being internet trolls, walking on eggshells at family holidays, and treating our employees, coworkers, siblings, parents, children, and neighbors like problems to solve rather than people to serve.

Whether we are aggressively fighting over the realities of our world (and our personal lives), completely avoiding facing them, or pretending like the tension of those realities doesn't exist, there is no doubt that we have lost the ability to communicate effectively and to deal with conflict.

―――――

If 2020 taught us anything, it is that there is no world in which we can exist where we can expect a conflict-free zone. And without honest conversation and connective communication, our relationships are impeded from maturing into their full potential. Even the healthiest relationships we have will contain tension; there will be disagreement, disappointments, and discouragement. How do we deal with that? How do we decide what we need to resolve, remove, and replace in our lives? How do we avoid a polarizing, isolating perspective that leaves us riddled with fear and anxiousness? How do we lean into mercy and the good news of grace?

Walter Brueggemann, my favorite Old Testament scholar, author, and activist, was interviewed on Krista Tippet's famous NPR podcast, *On Being*, in December 2018. He said:

> Phyllis Trible has taught us that the Hebrew word for mercy is the word for womb with different vowel points. So, mercy, she's suggested, is womb-like mother love. It is the capacity of a mother to totally give one's self over to the need and reality and

identity of the child. And mutatis mutandis, then, mercy is the capacity to give one's self away for the sake of the neighborhood.

Now, none of us do that completely. But it makes a difference if the quality of social transactions have to do with the willingness to give one's self away for the sake of the other, rather than the need to always be drawing all of the resources to myself for my own well-being. It is this kind of generous connectedness to others. And then I think our task is to see how that translates into policy. Now we're having huge political storms about whether our policies ought to reflect that kind of generosity to people other than us and people who are not as well-off as we are, or whatever.

I think that a community or a society, finally, cannot live without the quality of mercy. The problem for us is, what will initiate that? What will break the pattern of self-preoccupation enough to notice that the others are out there and that we are attached to them?[3]

I'm inviting you to reimagine the world as you know it. To consider what it would be like to live a more peaceful existence in which you think critically about your life, your relationships, and your place in the world. To recognize the generous mercy required to grasp the concept of interconnectedness to yourself, to God, to others up close and far away. To acknowledge all people—even those you or I disdain, disregard, or hate—are made in the image of God, worthy of love and mercy. To know with conviction that you have agency in the world. To understand conflict as a part of life but not the center of it. If you were in charge of the world for one day, what would you do to cultivate peace and mercy, to help others embody justice? In your own life, if you could reimagine one thing that would make all the difference, what would it be?

"Blessed are the peacemakers, for they will be called children of God" (Matt. 5:9).

ATTITUDE: My imagination is active and alive. Reality is what it is, but there is a better way, and God will help me see it.

AFFIRMATION: Conflict and tension are a normal part of life and relationships. I can learn skills that will help me manage conflict in a healthy way. I do not have to avoid it, and I do not have to live in a consistently volatile state, because I am a peacemaker and a child of God.

REFLECTION: Do I listen more to voices on social media, news, and YouTube than I listen to God and the people who love me most? What is the source of some of my biggest conflicts? What is leading me toward mercy?

TECHNIQUE: Normalize conflict and tension. Think about the various conflicts you may be facing or avoiding with family members, acquaintances, coworkers, and friends, online and in real life. What are you afraid of? What is the worst thing that could happen? Could you survive that? If you decide to engage, begin the dialogue by saying something like, "Difficult conversations are hard for me, but I care about our relationship, and this is important for us to do. I may not say everything the right way, but I will respect you. I am asking you to have grace for me, if I fumble over my words or need a minute to think. Thank you for being willing to be in this conflict with me."

CHAPTER 6

When Class, Gender, and Race Collide

W hen I think about the *why* behind our disagreements with each other, I also think about the "isms" I mentioned at the beginning of this book. There's a reason that premarital classes cover finances, gender roles, family culture and ethnicity, faith, and political affiliation. Because these are the things couples fight about. One person who usually feels like there will always be enough money marries someone who feels like there is never enough, and that's usually connected to their backgrounds—growing up with a lot or a little. Same with gender roles. Did Mom do homeboy's laundry and cook all his meals? Then it's not that unusual for him to expect his wife to do the same. One partner had access to private school and a paid-for college education while the other partner attended public school and struggled through college, working and paying bills. If they choose to have kids, they are then operating from different value systems and might argue about what's best for their children. Interracial couples might have to navigate newfound racism in family members. And for many couples, there is dread around holidays with the in-laws due to opposing political views or convictions of faith.

Like it or not, our class, gender, and race influence how we show up in the world and how we relate to and clash with people. Marriage is just one small example of this kind of collision. It's highly likely you've experienced something similar on your job or in your neighborhood, friendships, family, or faith community. I wish we weren't prone to ranking each other, but most of us are trained from birth to be this way. Assigning people by "Who is better and who is beneath?" can help us feel a sense of control and a sense of relief when we know our place or assign a place to others.

Throughout my own life, I've experienced a need to read the room in order to effectively engage or avoid tension and conflict. Do you do this? This is especially true for me when I'm punching above my weight class. Like when I'm the only woman in the boardroom, the only working mom at the park, out to a dinner where I'm the only one on a budget, one of the few willing to speak candidly, or perhaps the only person at the table without a degree. Imposter syndrome is real. Feelings of inadequacy, self-doubt, a sense that everyone is smarter than we are, and the inability to own our success can paralyze us. These feelings stem from our upbringing and experiences in the world. It would be great if this only happened to certain economic statuses, races, or genders, but these feelings come for us all, though to varying degrees depending on the former factors.

It is vital to our growth for us to understand why we do what we do. We work backward to move forward. Our past informs our present until we face it, deal with it, and heal it. That doesn't mean our instincts or fears will go away completely, but it does mean they no longer have control over our decisions and responses to life and circumstances. Let me illustrate this by sharing some of mine, with the hope that your own might become more visible to you.

When I am alone with a man, I sometimes worry he will try to take control of me or may try something sexually, because of the many times I've been objectified and sexually assaulted. When I am in a room where people wear $1,000 shoes and carry $3,000 handbags, I feel insecure because I did not grow up with that kind of money. It reminds me of feeling small as a teenager working at a country club, where I was sometimes treated poorly for being the help. It scares me to think that I might always be "the help," and I am tempted to shrink myself down so I'm in a place where the room ranking feels familiar again.

When I am in a meeting in which I'm watching another woman repeatedly being talked over or shut down, I feel nervous about speaking up and helping her use her voice, because I've been taught that women's voices are not as important as men's. It reminds me of the times I was told to shut up or called stupid when I tried to express my thoughts and ideas. When I find myself acting superior and looking down on someone because of who they are, what they have, or what they believe, I feel scared to admit and own that character flaw because it is embarrassing and shameful. The world taught me that the appearance of perfection is more important than humility and integrity. It reminds me of the times I have acted accepting and loving to a person in public yet rejected them in private.

As I continue to deal with my fears and teach myself new responses through my recovery journey, I'm growing in loving myself and others as made in the image of God. By rooting our identity in Christ, we learn to ignore the internal voices that tell us we don't belong, that rank us according to our race, economic status, or gender. In knowing the profound love of

Christ, we come to accept our brokenness, growing to believe that it's okay to make mistakes. In accepting the truth that our value is inherent and God-given, regardless of our economic status, skin color, nationality, or the parts between our legs, we are more readily able to outgrow the mentalities and perspectives we inherited. We can change. We do not have to rely on a job title, bank account, network, or partner to give us significance.

I wrote in my book *Rise of the Truth Teller,*

> I am significant, no matter my circumstances. I am someone even without any relational attachments or personal achievements. My value and dignity are inherent in the God who made me. I bear his image. I do not have to exhaust myself to please him or anybody else. And neither do you. We are significant. We are someone. You are the image of God on the earth. We don't have to prove ourselves.[1]

The more we internalize this truth, the less we'll need to rank ourselves or others in the human hierarchy and the more we'll see each other as equals. If we grow in our understanding of how class, race, and gender inform our thinking and our sense of belonging, then we are not bound by them.

But at times, the divide between us feels like a chasm. Too great of a gap to cross, too deep to try. Is there a bridge to understanding? To reciprocity? From our money to our choices to our gender, politics, skin color, and religion, we lack understanding and empathy for one another. I suspect we also lack the courage, or perhaps the energy, to try to step outside ourselves and our camps to understand and empathize. It is easier to settle back into what we know.

For the last several years, we've seen a collective pressing into a few of these gaps. While we have yet to have a full reckoning on the issue of class in America (or globally) and how it affects every sector of society—the way it separates people groups of every color and age—we have seen tangible progress in other areas. With the MeToo and TimesUp movements, we pressed into gender inequality. Men have been forced to give an account for their abuse of power in the workplace that resulted in women being sexually, emotionally, or otherwise abused. Church pastors and board members have been forced to resign for the mistreatment of women, and publicly women have taken to the streets to march and protest, beginning with the largest single-day protest in American history, on Inauguration Day in January 2017. Three million people marched in all fifty states and in thirty countries.[2]

The death of George Floyd in May 2020 and the subsequent global outpouring of solidarity for black and brown Americans seemed to press us further into the gap of inequality when it comes to race in America—at least for a time. Polarizing narratives certainly exist on both sides of the debate (and it is sad that black and brown lives are a debate in the first place), but books by Black authors have shot to the top of *New York Times* and Amazon bestseller lists. Men and women hungry to know more about racism and what they could do about it have tripled the social media following of many people of color engaged in educating the public about race and justice.

A concern of activists and allies in the racial justice community is, *Will this hunger to change last?* It's a valid question, and in August 2020 after Jacob Blake was shot seven times in the back in front of three of his four children, activist, poet, and rapper Propaganda posted a photo of the protest following that police shooting and wrote: "Y'all remember when the George Floyd sparked uprising started and y'all asked us if this moment felt different? Felt better? And we were *very* hesitant to say yes this moment was any different? Do you understand yet?"[3]

Will we see progress, or will we settle back into our camps and tribes, our comfort and security, our confirmed biases and our love for ideology?

———

Dr. Janet Helms has created the White Identity Model, with six steps of progress for Caucasian people to identify where they are on the spectrum of racial healing and justice: Contact, Disintegration, Reintegration, Pseudo-Independence, Immersion-Emersion, and Autonomy.[4] I've found it a very helpful tool to examine how we're moving along the path of becoming aware of racial injustice.

She describes the process of gaining autonomy from the camp we most securely identify with in order to identify other perspectives and ways of being in the world. First, at the Contact stage, an individual subscribes to a colorblind ethos of dealing with race. "I just don't see color" is their motto, and in fact, they may consider conversations about race as stirring up racism. Second, Disintegration happens when an experience or conversation demonstrates clearly that racism is real. This stage is marked by feelings of guilt and shame, and if these emotions are not channeled in a healthy way, Reintegration happens. Third, during Reintegration, the individual returns to the Contact stage, usually doubling down on their logic and even going so far as to blame victims for their plight in life. They may admit that as a White person they have privilege, but probably it is because they deserve it or in some way are superior to other minority groups.

Fourth, if a person overcomes this sense of superiority, they can move into the Pseudo-Independence stage, which is a positive racial identification. They begin to look to non-White people to uncover, understand, and confront racism, instead of looking only to themselves or other White people. But it is difficult at this stage for individuals to understand how they can be both anti-racist and White. Fifth, the next stage, Immersion-Emersion, is powerful, because the individual begins to connect to their own racial identity (what does it mean to be White?) and maintains the desire to be anti-racist, while also helping other White people connect to and grow in this desire. Finally, the Autonomy stage is reached in which an individual has a positive view of their own racial identity (no feelings of guilt or shame), has deep connections to others, actively pursues justice, and works to root out racism in their spheres of influence.

I believe that White America remains perpetually stuck between Disintegration and Reintegration. I've seen this so clearly in many people and pastors I love. A tragedy happens that wakes them up to the reality of racism; they are moved to action and change initially, but without a way to channel their anger or their feelings of guilt and shame, they reintegrate into their original camp and perspective about racism, sometimes doubling down and blaming minorities and victims for their experiences. For Christians, without education or real relationships to guide them, and without spiritual leaders to disciple them, their ideas of race tend to form from the media they consume and much of that is partisan in nature. In America, politics and religion seem to form the bedrock of our belief systems and sense of belonging in community. This makes it difficult to press beyond reintegration, into autonomy.

The presidential election of 2020 taught us that Americans are split nearly down the middle as holding values that line up with either the Democratic or Republican party, while the White evangelical church still showed almost 80 percent support for Donald Trump. In fact, there was a marginal increase of support for Trump from Black and Latinx Americans from 2016 to 2020, demonstrating that people groups are not a monolith.

There's so much more to say here about politics and religion, but it is telling that our discipleship in America led the majority of White Christians who self-identify as prizing morality to vote for a person with outstanding lawsuits for both sexual and financial crimes who brags about assaulting women, calls Mexicans rapists, shouts about building walls, and displays very clear racist and sexist behavior; who has led the world in setting terrible records during a pandemic; and who has dismissed everyone who didn't agree with him—not a shining example for Christians. Perhaps we are used to men like Trump, or a politer version of him, leading our churches. The Bible has even been used to explain away such crushing rhetoric, such as the story of David or King Cyrus being applied to make a case that, as "God's chosen man," all bad behavior can be excused. Roles in government and in ministry, where people are called to serve, morph into roles where there is a culture of silence, shame, and control. With a team of folks complicit in the culture, the leader gets away with abusing power.

The gender gap in opportunity, benefits, and pay causes women to suppress concerns, to struggle to speak up, or even to defend the indefensible, and, with no accountability, men justify and carry on with their behavior. In many conservative churches, abortion is a main issue driving political choices, and some even teach that to vote for a Democrat means you are not a Christian. In more progressive churches the opposite is true. I believe the church needs to do right by people, but to accuse someone of not being Christian because of how they chose to exercise their democratic right to vote is problematic indeed. Kristin Kobes Du Mez, author of *Jesus and John Wayne: How White Evangelicals Corrupted a Faith and Fractured a Nation*, wrote,

> For conservative White evangelicals, the "good news" of the Christian gospel has become inextricably linked to a staunch

commitment to patriarchal authority, gender difference, and Christian nationalism, and all of these are intertwined with White racial identity. Many Americans who now identify as evangelicals are identifying with this operational theology—one that is Republican in its politics and traditionalist in its values.[5]

This is hard for me to understand because I didn't grow up in a faith community that told me how to think or how to vote, and in our household, critical thinking about elections was welcomed. My parents rarely voted the same as each other. My family members belong to Republican, Democrat, and Independent parties, but without the Christian influence. There was no enmeshment of politics and faith, and therefore, politics were a normal part of our civic life, not the sum total of our beliefs about God or each other.

It was a shock to my system, in my early thirties, to discover that in some Christian schools, Sunday schools, and church services, people are actually taught they should vote for the Republican party because of abortion. They are taught to put America first, and their theology often does not include tending to the suffering or injustice of the poor or marginalized, or the racism and sexism that are often implicitly centered in the community. Constituents in evangelical churches can hold a strong groupthink due to the culture of their local church, and stepping out of turn in word or deed, even changing their mind about beliefs, comes at great cost to reputation and relationship. These potential losses greatly affect our ability to be honest and stay true to our convictions when they change. Dr. Helms's model teaches us that it is easy for us to be pulled back into our camps, especially when faith is the driving force behind our ability to believe racism is a problem in the first place. Quickly, we return to old ways of thinking because achieving autonomy would require we go against the grain of our relationships. We are creatures of habit who do not like rejection, and we fear the liminal spaces between one place and the next. Our desire for comfort and familiarity can drive us away from where we'd hoped to go and who we'd hoped to become.

Perhaps we resist moving into new ways of thinking and living because we fear losing family members, friends, and our sense of belonging in community if we change our minds about our beliefs and values. While this is certainly true sometimes, it is not *always* true. If we grow in handling conflict and the tension of transition, it becomes easier to engage in the necessary conversations required through the process of an evolving belief system. I've changed my mind about 208,606 times and kept nearly all of the people I love the most close. Have I lost relationships? Yes. Has it been worth it to stop letting the approval of people determine what I believe and who I become? Also yes.

━━━

Interdependent with the issue of race is class, which is something we feel all the time in America, though we struggle to name it or deal with it. America falsely teaches that we all have the same opportunities, and that pulling yourself up by your bootstraps works. There's a "Look at all I went through and still I'm living the dream—you can too, if you work hard and trust God" vibe that is without substance. Women, BIPOC, and poor people of every nationality and ethnicity should not have to be an exception to the rule in order to succeed in life. Nancy Isenberg, author of the must-read book *White Trash: The 400-Year Untold Story of Class in America*, wrote, "How does a culture that prizes equality of opportunity explain, or indeed accommodate, its persistently marginalized people? Twenty-first-century Americans need to confront this enduring conundrum. Let us recognize the existence of our underclass."[6]

In thinking about how to confront this issue, I wonder if Dr. Helms's model of how we move along the spectrum of identity and race could also work when it comes to class. The glaring difference between class and race, or class and gender, is that skin color and sex are identifiable in the majority of people immediately. Generational wealth and economic status are not always obvious in our initial encounters with people. Still, we do not talk about class enough in America and how it impacts our relationships with others.

The National Bureau of Economic Research recently released a study that highlights the difficulty of Americans ever moving beyond the class they are born into.[7] This was one of the first economic studies done that included wealth from previous generations as a factor in class and social mobility. Not only do children from families with generational wealth inherit land or monetary gain that enables them to purchase their first homes or invest in the stock market, but they are also given the intellectual knowledge necessary to navigate the upper echelons of the world, such as how to utilize the stock market, how money works, and how to save and prepare for the future. With access to relational networks, generational connections open up a world of internships, career advice, and recommendations for potential roles in their desired field. Ana Swanson, in an article for the *Washington Post*, wrote about the study:

> Research by economists from Harvard and Berkeley found that fewer than 10 percent of people in the bottom fifth of the wealth distribution will make it into the top fifth. Things weren't much better for the middle class: Only about 20 percent of people in the middle fifth would rise into the top fifth over the course of their lives.[8]

Is that because all people of a lower class are lazy, broke, welfare queens, or trailer trash—or does this have more to do with an implicit social order we are not allowed to break? Is it perhaps more connected to minimum wage jobs, where survival is the primary goal and saving is impossible even in a good month with overtime? Is there an inherent disrespect or disdain for the American working class that discourages advancement and equality? And if all of these are a *yes*, does that not drastically affect how we view and relate to each other?

Let's stop and think for a moment about the places in our lives where we are present with others who are not in our economic class. I think of classrooms, faith communities, sporting events, libraries, and parks. I also think of office buildings, restaurants, and stores. In all these scenarios, we are either alone or attending with family and friends; working with or working for others; being served or serving in a particular role. So, how often are we in environments together where we are not divided? Is it possible for us to relate to each other outside of the social hierarchy that class creates? And if not, what does this say about our gospel? What story does this tell about our love for God and our judgments about each other?

———

Part of the reason we lack understanding around the intersection of social issues is because of the splitting public discourse. Conservative politicians, pundits, and preachers tend to teach people with fear-based rhetoric—that intersectionality is an issue of critical race theory, or something only feminists and Marxists are concerned with. This is dangerous because we tend to dismiss what's true about ideas and, therefore, what's true about us. This can lead to a false sense of unity as we double down on the ideas we believe are right, to the detriment of diversity and opportunities for personal growth.

On the flip side, liberal politicians, pundits, and preachers tend to sound elitist and condescending, demanding near-perfect agreement and behavior in order to colabor. Not only is this impossible but it can be difficult for people in a process of growth to feel like they are ever doing anything right. This keeps people from seeing any truth in a theory they might find disagreeable or recognizing that the intersection of class, race, and gender is actually a tender place where strong solidarity is possible.

Sometimes, I want to scream when I read some of the perspectives of those in power from both sides of the aisle. What I want to say to them emphatically is this: You are so clearly *not* in relationship with anyone who is actually poor, or making minimum wage, or living paycheck to paycheck as a middle-class person in America. You have *no idea* what it's like to be a woman with wealth but no power or a mother living below the poverty line, and you have *no idea* how race compounds this issue.

I remember asking my mom about the feminist movement in the '70s and '80s. She said, "Oh, honey, that movement wasn't for me. I was working at the mill, going to school, with little kids. When was I supposed to march in the streets?" This is why whole books exist on White feminism, why many women of color do not identify with the word *feminism*, and why women like my mom don't either. As often is the case, the movement centered on wealthier White women and left out lower economic classes, women of color, and conservative pro-life women. When we refuse to recognize how gender, race, and class collide, people are absent—left out and left behind. Isn't it easy to see how people who should be allies can instead become enemies?

———

It is rare, though not impossible, to find people from different economic classes, races, and genders seated at the table with decision makers across all sectors of society, including the church. In government, religious institutions, real estate development, health care and insurance, education administration, food distribution, and more, people decide outcomes for others without one ounce of input from those directly impacted. All. The. Time.

We can do better, and in the long run, effective collaboration leads to more meaningful work, individual integrity, and communal wholeness.

Christians must do the hard work of minding the messy middle, where most people live, instead of shouting at each other from the most polarizing points. Unity is possible when we seek to understand one another, share our stories, and avoid the judgments we are quick to make. It takes us leaning into love, not other people's opinions or our own offense or cynicism, in order to accept each other rather than assume our biases and preferences are true. We do have common ground, but when we allow everything to disciple us but Jesus Christ, it feels harder to find. People are amazing, truly, and with candid, kind, grown-up conversations, we can recognize the image of God in others.

And when we can't? When there is no reasonable way forward? Well, we move on.

There is a lie we believe in churches, which is that we need to be friends with everyone—that reconciliation means we must please people or they must please us, and then we'll fix the relationship and move on with our lives. When it comes to unsafe, toxic people, what can we fix? Unless there is mutual respect and a desire for safe, honest, accountable relationship, there is no way forward. Romans 13 tells us to "Let no debt remain outstanding, except the continuing debt to love one another" (v. 8). Sometimes, it's as simple as, *I love you with the love of the Lord, but I don't like you much, okay; and let's get real, you don't like me either.* We are not friends. Reconciliation is not possible here.

We must mature enough to walk away from our camps, from any belief systems we discover are hindering our relationships and keeping us from becoming more like Christ. If devaluing women, the poor, or people of other races and nationalities is a value in your camp, it's time to break away from those mindsets. If you discover yourself on the extreme end of anything but love, it's time to reevaluate. Yes, this will take incredible courage, but that's the gospel of Jesus Christ. Faith to change, faith to grow, faith to sing, "Though none go with me, still I will follow. No turning back, no turning back."

Is autonomy from our tribes, factions, familiarities, self-serving beliefs, and societal sects possible? Does our relationship with Jesus propel us toward that end? Let's explore that next.

ATTITUDE: My heart is open to learning.

AFFIRMATION: I am capable of loving, and being loved, beyond my limitations. When God stirs my heart toward something new, it is not unreasonable for me to feel fear or to struggle to leave what feels familiar. Fear does not have to hinder my ability to embrace both the community I come from and the people I'm learning to love.

REFLECTION: Do I exercise full autonomy from the people I belong to? Why or why not?

TECHNIQUE: Sit and work through the steps in Dr. Helms's Identity Model. Where do you see yourself now? Ask the Holy Spirit if that is truly where you are. Receive his grace. Where would you like to be? Trust that you can change.

CHAPTER 7

Autonomy from Our Camp

Is autonomy from our camps possible? As we seek to answer this question, it is important to examine if Scripture addresses the concerns we share around the issues of race, gender, and class. Is God concerned about these things, or are we getting "too political"? Does he want us to settle into our tribes, or do we need to push ourselves toward communities that are richer and more diverse in nature? If Jesus really is our peace, and has destroyed the barrier and the dividing wall of hostility between our groups in order to reconcile us to God through the cross, and if all of us together have equal access to the Father by the Spirit,[1] then why isn't this a pillar to our development of discipleship within our places of belonging?

If we are meant to be one, why does the church as a whole not spend more time addressing what divides us and thoughtfully working to cultivate wholeness and health across our various backgrounds, economic realities, nationalities, and genders? Why are we known more for what we are against and who we hate than what we are for and who we love? Must we continue to define things in the polarizing words of this world, or can we transition to seeing people as made in the image of God, neighbors we are commanded to love?

From beginning to end, the Bible is full of instruction on how we can love God, ourselves, and our neighbor. This is crucial to autonomy and healthy differentiation from others. Originally, the Ten Commandments helped establish covenant community among the people of God. I believe this is why they begin with the commandment to have no other gods before the Lord, no idols or graven images. When God is God in our life, when we magnify him, focus on his holiness, receive his grace and forgiveness, and cultivate a life of worship, confession, and repentance, we are positioned to not take his name in vain. By this I mean we will not use Jesus to further our agenda, to push people out of his presence, to perpetuate hate even as we say we believe that God is love, or to act like God is one way when we know he is not.

Then the commandments go on to explain what we do not want to do to our neighbors: stealing, adultery, jealousy, killing, and so forth. This should be basic knowledge, but I think we all know common sense is not all that common, since we still struggle with nearly everything on this list. And lest we think we are exempt from acting a fool, Jesus comes along and is like, "Hey, if you even hate someone in your heart, you've committed murder. If you've lusted at all after anyone, you've committed adultery." Does he do this to shame us? I don't think so, but I do think perhaps he wants us to stop thinking we are better than other people who commit more visible sins against their neighbors, because he knows what's going on in our hearts. And while we might never actually murder anyone, or steal from a person we're jealous of, or sleep with someone we probably shouldn't, he wants us to know that he knows we want to do it. He equates what's happening inside to what's happening outside. This is about integrity, not just in action and behavior, which in general religious people are very proud of, but also in heart and mind, which religious people are less likely to admit and own.

I'm a firm believer in recovery communities for this reason. We start with story; we lead with our brokenness, knowing that if we don't share the awful crap inside our heads, it has the potential to wreck our sobriety. When David cries out, in Psalm 51, a prayer of repentance for and ownership of his personal failures (also actual murder and adultery), he says, "Behold You desire truth in the inward parts, and in the hidden part, You will make me to know wisdom" (v. 6 NKJV). Until he was confronted about his sin by the court prophet Nathan, David lived in denial about what he'd done to get what he wanted. He lusted after, sent for, and raped Bathsheba. Then, when he learned he'd gotten her pregnant, David commanded his generals to send her husband, Uriah, to the front lines of war, where he was sure to be killed. This same husband was such a man of integrity that he refused to leave his men or enjoy any pleasure with his wife (David's first hope for not being found out in the affair), and he would not let his guard down for a moment while serving his country and his king.[2]

The circumstances for Bathsheba and Uriah were severe, as were the consequences for David. After Uriah's death, Bathsheba was taken to the palace to be David's wife, and their baby did not live but died, as Nathan had prophesied.

David moved out of denial and into a place of reflection and lament, which led to his confession and repentance. The instructions of Jesus regarding our internal world are a clear reminder that we are a people in denial. This denial is a problem. We are trapped in our judgment of others, blind to our own sin and the evil lurking within us. And yes, I said evil.

Why are we so obsessed with our own purity and with what we would *never* do that so-and-so does? Do we need the cross or not? We are not pure; we are far from perfect, and it is time to own that, to stop obsessing with a self-help gospel focused on personal purity and perfection and instead embrace the good news of grace, which is that our righteousness is filthy rags. All have "sinned and fall short of the glory of God" (Rom. 3:23 ESV). There is no distinction between those who sin out loud and those who sin in secret, between thought and deed. And we "are justified by his grace as a gift, through the redemption that is in Christ Jesus, whom God put forward as a propitiation by his blood, to be received by faith" (v. 25 ESV). What God did on the cross showed that he is both "just and the justifier of the one who has faith in Jesus" (v. 26 ESV).

If we held this firm as a conviction of our faith, we'd not only be better Christians but better neighbors. People who are in tune with their own brokenness and who release themselves from the shame of not being (or pretending to be) perfect tend to connect more deeply to others. They are more able to suspend judgment, hold healthy expectations, and carry a growth mindset, and they can move through life more liberally and without reproach. They are also more successful at resolving conflict with themselves and others. People at peace with themselves can find contentment no matter their circumstances and can better engage in discussion around difficult or polarizing topics.

———

So, what does the Bible say about race? About class? The human race is mentioned six times in the Old Testament, referring to our whole species. The Bible does not categorize based on skin color but on language, tribe, or nation. Defining people by their skin color is relatively new, although we can see hints of this in Scripture. In the Song of Solomon, as one example, the protagonist is a female who shares her fear that she will not be loved by her partner because her job working in the fields has darkened her skin.[3] This is a place where we see her gender, race, and class intersect.

Another example is the Samaritan woman at the well with Jesus. Her gender, ethnicity, past, and religion disqualified her from the boundaries of society's norms. Through her interaction with Jesus in John 4, we see how God loves women of all races, even those with complicated pasts and different religions. Jesus says, "If you have seen me, you have seen the Father" (John 14:9 CEV). His connections and interactions with people help us understand who and how God loves.

As a final example, in Acts 10 and 11, the apostle Peter dreams the same dream, three times, about eating unclean food. He refuses three times to eat it (three-peat denial is kind of Peter's thing), and just before he wakes, he hears, "Do not call something unclean if God has made it clean" (Acts 10:15 NLT). Next thing he knows, there's a knock at the door, with an invitation for Peter to visit a Roman centurion named Cornelius. God spoke to Cornelius and told him where to send his men, and that Peter would come to tell these gentiles about Jesus.

As Cornelius was praying, an angel had appeared to him, telling him, "Your prayers and gifts to the poor have been received by God as an offering!" (v. 4 NLT). How powerful is it that this is what moved the heart of God toward Cornelius? We see here that God cares about those who are at a severe disadvantage in our communities, and those with the means to do something about it are seen by God.

Peter, prejudiced against gentiles and likely also against Roman officers in government, realized through the repetition of the visions that God does not reject anyone because of their race, class, or gender. Peter, a Jew, was not superior to Cornelius, a gentile. Because of this revelation, Peter goes into the house, against his custom, and tells this community about Christ. Marveling, Peter tells them straight off, "I see very clearly that God shows no favoritism. In every nation he accepts those who fear him and do what is right. This is the message of Good News for the people of Israel—that there is peace with God through Jesus Christ, who is Lord of all" (vv. 34–36 NLT). All the people are baptized, and Peter stays on in the home for several days.

But the good news does not stop there. Peter then heads home to Jerusalem, where he is confronted by people who argue with him about having eaten in the home of people who were not circumcised. Peter's like, "Look, I know, my religion made me a racist bigot too, but what happened was, God gave me a vision." He then explains to them the leading of the Holy Spirit, and says, "Who was I to stand in God's way?" (11:17 NLT). Their response? "They stopped objecting and began praising God. They said, 'We can see that God has also given the Gentiles the privilege of repenting of their sins and receiving eternal life" (v. 18 NLT).

Not only did God help Peter overcome his own prejudice, but in the process, Peter was able to minister the Holy Spirit to people hungry for him and lead some of his own people out of their bias and racism as well. This is why I'm a firm believer in not divorcing completely from the camps we come from. As we cross over into autonomy, it is important to remember that God cares about the bondage of those we love who still share the beliefs we used to hold. There may be a time of separation, and even permanent severance from some relationships that are unsafe for us to return to, but there will also be people who will watch us grow and change and who will one day receive the freedom God has given us.

Superiority in any form is bondage. Racism, colorblindness, sexism, and classism are dangerous traps that keep us from experiencing the fullness of God and bury hatred for humanity in our heart. Make no mistake: this is sin. And it does not please God.

There is a way out. First Corinthians 10:13 says, "No temptation has overtaken you except what is common to mankind. And God is faithful; he will not let you be tempted beyond what you can bear. But when you are tempted, he will also provide a way out so that you can endure it." You don't have to live this way. God will provide a way out, as he did with Peter, first through the repeating vision and then through a real and personal encounter with a good human named Cornelius—and as the Lord did for all of Peter's friends who scolded him for that choice.

Peter probably didn't know he was racist. But his religion had raised him to think that even entering the home of someone who didn't look like him, live like him, or believe like him was a sin. For him to eat with an uncircumcised gentile was unheard of! But God is faithful.

Many Christians critique me for my passion for the Black Lives Matter movement, and yes, I am a fan of the organization as well. You know why? Because I have actual friends who are in leadership there, and they love Jesus. With all their hearts. Passionately! Their work in cities across America is helping us understand more about the marginalization of people because of their race, class, and gender. Is it a perfect organization? No, but is your church? Also no. It burns my biscuits when this organization is painted as a Marxist, communist institution that Christians should not support or care about. I hope God gives you a vision and tells you not to call unclean what he calls clean, and I hope you listen to the voices of those who are sitting at the table eating, in homes, with people who are actually in the movement.

As Peter asked about himself, I ask us, Who are we to stand in God's way? He is not bound by our religious and political beliefs. Let's stop acting like the Holy Spirit will only move where we think he should move.

————

Ken Wytsma, in his book *The Myth of Equality*, goes into great detail about where the concept of race began, since it is only mentioned six times in the Old Testament.[4] This information and teaching can also be studied by reading the work of Native American teachers and activists such as the late Pastor Richard Twiss and Mark Charles, who have dedicated their lives to helping us understand the Doctrine of Discovery.

Essentially, the construct of race cannot be clearly defined historically in art, literature, poetry, or philosophy until the 1500s. This was also the time European colonialism really gathered steam in its exploration and conquering of other lands. Though, of course, conquering and being conquered had virtually always been happening tribally, nationally, and biblically, domination and subjugation through a racial hierarchy was not a thing—until the church began to send out its leadership to take land.

The Doctrine of Discovery began with Papal Bulls of the fifteenth century that gave Christian explorers the right to lay claim to lands they "discovered" on behalf of their Christian monarchs. Any land that was not inhabited by Christians was available to be "discovered," claimed, and exploited. If the "pagan" inhabitants could be converted, they might be spared. If not, they could be enslaved or killed.[5] In 1493, Pope Alexander VI issued a Papal Bull that authorized Spain and Portugal to colonize the Americas and convert and enslave its native peoples as subjects. And King Ferdinand of Spain sent out Christopher Columbus to discover the Americas.

This is what I mean when I say that religion can teach us to hate. Particularly when religion marries politics, because the love child of pride and greed is always violence. Can you imagine your pastor telling you, "Go on ahead and go to that town. Wherever you set your foot is territory God's given you. Get people saved by telling them the 'good news,' and if they don't convert, or they resist you, go on and kill them, rape them, enslave them. It's their fault for not complying. You're in charge."

What!? Are we insane? Also, why wouldn't the first response for a Christian be, "NOPE. NOT TODAY, SATAN." Also, "You belong to your father, the devil, and you want to carry out your father's desires. He was a murderer from the beginning, not holding to the truth, for there is no truth in him. When he lies, he speaks his native language, for he is a liar and the father of lies" (John 8:44).

But isn't this what still happens? In militias across America who are ready to kill if necessary. In police forces who show up with tanks and riot gear for unarmed citizens. In households where abuse happens to children who "brought it on themselves." We twist our hate into love of God and country and call it good.

I cannot say it better than Catholic activist, teacher, and author Jane Elliot, who was asked on Al Jazeera America News, "Why do we hate?" Her response:

> We hate because we are taught to hate. We hate because we are ignorant. We are the product of ignorant people, who have been taught an ignorant thing, which is that there are four or five different races. There are not four or five different races. There's only one race on the face of the Earth, and we're all members of that race, the human race, but we have separated people into races so that some of us can see ourselves as superior to the others. We thought it would work, I guess; it hasn't worked, it has been bad for everyone. . . . There is no gene for racism. There is no gene for bigotry. You're not born a bigot; you have to learn to be a bigot. Anything you learn, you can unlearn. It's time to

unlearn our bigotry. I'm an educator, and it is my business as an educator to lead people out of ignorance. The ignorance of thinking you're better or worse than someone else because of the amount of a pigment in your skin. Pigmentation in your skin has nothing to do with intelligence or with your worth as a human being. It's time to get over that.[6]

In Genesis 1, God demonstrates that he feels similarly; he creates the human race, communicating his highest and best for us to exercise dominion on the earth as those made in his image. To our Creator, we are equal in his eyes regardless of our skin color, gender, size, ableism, national status, or any other way society may choose to rate us. The ground is truly level at the foot of the cross.

Since the 1500s, the social construct of race has been used to uphold the supremacy of the White race and to subjugate, enslave, and even kill people of other races. And while we tend to think of this as a Black and White issue in America, we see Native American people groups enslaved and killed, their families separated even up until the 1960s through compulsory boarding schools. We see Chinese exclusion acts, Japanese internment camps from 1942 to 1945, migrant children at our borders sleeping on floors and in cages throughout several presidencies, and so much more. There is a hierarchy in our society, enforced through political and religious systems and found in health care, education, housing, and more. It directly affects us, hurts us, or harms us based on our race. Without autonomy, we (Caucasian people especially) continue to perpetuate these injustices.

Ken Wytsma also writes in *The Myth of Equality*,

Due to our sin nature, human beings are bound to fall far short of creating social systems and governments that recognize and fully honor the biblical doctrine of human equality. Instead, we discriminate and devalue people on the basis of gender, skin color, mental capacity, functional capability, age, citizenship, and other traits.

The New Testament reiterates the concept that all humanity is equal. A new commitment to abolish walls of division flows out of the incarnation, teachings, death, and resurrection of Jesus. Thus the apostle Peter can say, "I now realize how true it is that God does not show favoritism" (Acts 10:34). Paul writes the same to the church in Rome (Romans 2:11), and James warns against showing partiality (James 2:1, 9). For the early followers of Christ, this idea of the unity of all humanity was radically countercultural; nonetheless, Paul expresses it clearly in his letter to the Galatians: "There is neither Jew nor Gentile, neither slave nor free, nor is there male and female, for you are all one in Christ Jesus" (Galatians 3:28).

There can be no mistake: in creating the world, God ultimately intended that we all be valued equally. The church in the age of exploration missed this, and the American church in the age of Manifest Destiny missed this as well.[7]

So, in this way, the responsibility lies with us, as Christians, to better understand the systems of this world that we might discover a biblical way of thinking about each other, relating to each other, serving one another, and loving each other that is not solely based on race, class, or gender. And if one of our brothers or sisters is held in bondage because of the color of their skin, then we are also not free and must move to act with compassion and justice.

Walter Brueggemann said this at the Justice Conference in Portland, Oregon, in 2011:

One of the misfortunes in the long history of the church is that we have mistakenly separated love of God from love of neighbor and always they are held together in prophetic poetry. Covenant members who practice justice and righteousness are to be active advocates for the vulnerable and the marginalized and people without resources. And that then becomes the way to act out and exhibit one's love of God.

So love of God gets translated into love of vulnerable neighbors. And the doing of justice is the prophetic invitation to do what needs to be done to enable the poor and the disadvantaged and the neglected to participate in the resources and wealth of the community.

And injustice is the outcome of having skewed neighborly processes so some are put at an unbearable disadvantage. And the Gospel invitation is that people intervene in that to correct those mistaken arrangements.[8]

The idea of a gospel invitation to correct the arrangements within our communities that create unbearable circumstances appeals to me. We are often sold a bill of goods in Christianity that is unbiblical. Following Jesus should not be easy (it's a narrow road, remember?), and when we are bored or idle we begin to act selfishly. We focus on our comfort, our needs, our rights. We've all seen those Christians out in these streets who act the fool, who fight online like it's their full-time job, complaining about the most ridiculous things.

Christians actually care about others. Personal salvation is a wonderful start but insufficient over a lifetime of walking with Christ. We are to actively participate in engaging with people outside our boxes and camps, per the Gospels. With autonomy, we belong to Jesus, who is Lord, and we love people, who are no longer our lord. This freedom that comes from grace empowers us to root ourselves in connections with others that allow us to hold our convictions without compromise.

I wonder if our resistance to autonomy—and the reason we break from our camps temporarily only to reintegrate again after some difficulty (rejection, mocking, judgment, etc.)—is because we are resistant to conflict and change. Honest conversations with direct dialogue are difficult. To say the truth without a bitter edge, to express our desire to grow and change even if it offends or hurts people we love, takes an incredible amount of courage.

Many of us secure our identity in the ideology and approval of our tribe, even if it is toxic, unhealthy, or simply not serving us or Christ, rather than securing our identity in God. We struggle to get over the disapproval of others and push through the discomfort of beginning to belong elsewhere, during the in-between of where we were and where we hope to be. Part of making strong choices to transition as necessary in life is deciding to not live in denial, to deal in reality, and to make decisions accordingly.

Russian philosopher and writer Fyodor Dostoevsky said, "Above all, don't lie to yourself. The man who lies to himself and listens to his own lie comes to a point where he cannot distinguish the truth within him or around him, and so loses respect for himself. And having no respect, he ceases to love."[9] Can someone call the fire department? Because Dostoevsky lit the whole place on fire with this word.

———

What does it take for us to change? What causes us to care about the pain of others enough to be moved with compassion? Something must jolt us awake. A cataclysmic event makes us so painfully aware of reality that we can no longer live in denial. The incarceration and torture of women in the suffrage movement. Emmett Till. Fannie Lou Hamer's speech at the 1964 Democratic Convention, which was so powerful that President Lyndon B. Johnson moved quickly to host a press conference so that national news wouldn't cover it. (This backfired though, because they kept playing it on repeat.) The Vietnam War.

Sandy Hook. 9/11. Occupy Wall Street. Trayvon Martin's murder. Kalief Browder's suicide. The Chibok schoolgirls kidnapping by Boko Haram. Alan Kurdi, the three-year-old Syrian refugee who washed up dead on a Turkish beach resort shore. The arrest of Filipino journalist Maria Ressa in 2018. The executive order that legalized the separation of children from their parents (even breastfeeding infants) at the border between the United States and Mexico. Coronavirus. George Floyd.

We wake from our slumber, the sedative of security worn off long enough for us to see, to really see, our own condition, the condition of the world and that of our neighbor. We become ready to love. Perhaps we are horrified or angry, convicted of our complicity or silence, and we make a move to break away from the ideology or belief system dominant within our group. We courageously speak up at the dinner table or risk sharing a political idea that differs from those of our loved ones. We interpret Scripture about women or immigrants or justice or race in light of God's mercy—and we are mocked, shamed, or shunned. In our faith community, we speak thoughtfully to leadership about how to engage the relevant topics of our day—and we are met with talk of cultivating unity or told that pursuing these things is not biblical.

The cost of sharing our convictions, the potential (or literal) loss of relationship, the shame that comes from rejection, the conflicts that suddenly seem to surround us, are enough for the majority of us to shrink right back into who we were before we woke up. And as Dostoevsky says, we cease to love.

What will it take? How do we cross over into keeping a healthy attachment with people who no longer share or support our changing beliefs? How do we journey with people who have developed their belief system? How do we manage the tension from "here to there," that uncomfortable middle space of becoming? Is it possible to transition into a fully independent person capable of holding tension, complexity, and love for others in tandem with our convictions?

————

Communication skills are learned. We are not born with them, and most people do not grow up with great examples of engaging in healthy conflict. Most of us are a good combination of avoiding it like the plague and doing the exact opposite. But we can learn to do this.

Relationships require courage. More energy is needed than we imagine when we start them. More grace and mercy are necessary than we knew we had the capacity to give. But it's worth it. When you find your people, you find your life bubbling over with meaning and assurance. To be seen and known, to be loved as we are on our way to who we're becoming, is a sweet respite in this world. For someone to give us the privilege of knowing and loving them the same way is a gift. If we press into the tensions, deal with conflict as it arises, and remain curious about differences, then intimacy and connection in our homes, workplaces, churches, and friendship circles increases with transformative, life-giving power.

Courage does not mean we won't feel afraid; it means we will do what's necessary in spite of our fear. If it means giving up a religious conviction we discover is harmful or unbiblical, we do it—afraid. If it means we lose relational capital with people who are important to us, we do it—afraid. If it means having the difficult conversation we've been avoiding, we do it—afraid. If it means not exploding to avoid the intimacy of a healthy confrontation, we do it—afraid. If it means standing strong in the middle space of a changing belief system, we do it—afraid.

Disciples are learners. We were created to change and grow, as we learn. As Maya Angelou is often quoted as saying, "I did then what I knew to do. Now that I know better, I do better."[10]

Autonomy is possible, if we are willing to leave behind who we were to embrace life beyond our limitations.

ATTITUDE: When I know better, I will do better.

AFFIRMATION: I am a disciple. I am a learner. God can help me understand myself, other people, and the world he created. Even when I feel afraid, I can do what is right and necessary in spite of my fear.

REFLECTION: We need courage to confront in order to achieve autonomy. What in my past, or in my "camp," am I afraid to confront?

TECHNIQUE: Share your fears. When it comes to growing in community and belonging, as well as autonomy, we need to share our fears with trustworthy people who will encourage us to grow. Who can help you process your fears, particularly around race, class, and gender? Be as honest as you can—deal in reality, so real growth and real change are possible.

CHAPTER 8

For Lack of Justice
There Is Waste

I n January 2019, Netflix released a documentary called *The Biggest Little Farm*. John and Molly Chester were living in Santa Monica, California, where Molly worked as a private chef and her partner, John, as a cameraman and filmmaker. The couple decided to adopt a dog, and this dog refused to not bark all day long while they were away at work. Eventually, facing eviction, they decided to pursue their lifelong dream of owning a farm. After developing a business plan, the Chesters purchased two hundred acres of barren farmland in Moorpark, California, and devoted themselves to revitalizing the land.

Alongside other farmers, and their mentor Alan York, Molly and John brought a lifeless farm back from the dead through cultivating rich diversity in plants and animals. Instead of following the modern farming practice of monocropping—growing only one crop with great market efficiency at great expense to the earth—they sought to follow the natural progression of life, death, and interconnectedness within creation. Over eight years, investing more work and money than they planned, they solved problems with natural solutions, harnessed the power of permaculture, and even found ways to protect plants and animals against predators without killing them.

The neural pathways started firing across my brain as I watched this documentary from my airplane seat—as I watched creation make a clear case for complexity and diversity. *This is what God intended*, I thought to myself. Perhaps this hit me so hard because I constantly try to make sense of the beloved body of Christ, in all its various streams and expressions, and desperately try to understand why so few communities remain vitally strong in the complexities of the human experience. From ethnicity to class to gender to nationality to political affiliation, it is rare to discover a faith community ready and willing to harness the strength of diversity, to support structures that care for the vulnerable and empower people toward service and sacrifice, and to refuse to kill off or cancel even the enemy.

Did Jesus not have Judas at his table? Did he not also welcome a tax collector who worked for the oppressive Roman government, two sisters learning to love, a woman who poured a year's worth of her wages onto his feet, fishermen who were not exactly the ideal deacons? Did he not tell the children to come to him? Did he not also heal the sick, cast out demons from those who were tortured and self-harming, touch the leper, and maintain a piercing love for those society discarded or considered undeserving of existence? Aside from the religious leaders who cloaked their spiritual oppression in their maintenance of the law, who did Jesus shun? Who did he send away? Did class or any other metric hinder his welcome into belonging in the kingdom of God?

As Canadian American author, speaker, and theologian Ronald Rolheiser says,

The church is always God hung between two thieves. Thus, no one should be surprised or shocked at how badly the church has betrayed the gospel and how much it continues to do so today. It had never done very well. Conversely, however, nobody should deny the good the church has done either. It has carried grace, produced saints, morally challenged the planet, and made, however imperfectly, a house for God to dwell in on this earth.

To be connected with the church is to be associated with scoundrels, warmongers, fakes, child molesters, murderers, adulterers, and hypocrites of every description. It also, at the same time, identifies you with the saints and the finest persons of heroic soul within every time, country, race, and gender. To be a member of the church is to carry the mantle of both the worst sin and the finest heroism of soul . . . because the church always looks exactly as it looked at the original crucifixion, God hung among thieves.[1]

It is unsettling to watch Christians in America ruthlessly pursue their safety and security, demonize and belittle those who disagree, and seek a cosigner for beliefs that are not only unbiblical but anti-Christ and anti-creation. It is also alarming to watch believers push further into camps and echo chambers, centering our belief systems outside the love of Christ. Is our way of living cultivating the beloved community of Christ—God among thieves? Or are we dividing the church into factions, communities centered on whether or not we agree?

═══

As I learn more about modern farming practices here in the United States, I can't help but draw a parallel to the journey of the Western evangelical church. Bigger, better, and more; high production; a strategic focus on outcomes and numbers; equipment for a service over equipping the saints. In this model, churches burn through staff, volunteers, and others to achieve goals, and as these people leave or are pushed out of the community because they are tired or have questions, the church loses relationships and reputation in order to preserve its image of production. Not people.

To further draw the comparison, monoculture is the key to the function of these churches. There is a sameness—not a oneness, but a sameness. Even in multicultural churches there tends to be one ethos, one dominant culture found in the worship, the messages, the stories and quotes used in illustrations, the missions work, and the position of female leadership, and this ethos is almost always that of the male leader. (I married a pastor, by the way. I know the work it takes for a man not to center himself in the congregation and mission of the church. It's rare for men.)

So, the faith community does one thing: produce. The same thing. Over and over again. The formula repeats itself through networks, conferences, resources, and books, and across the landscape churches are large spiritual farms offering only one fruit to the people who are lonely, dried up, striving, and serving, with little yield of relationship and redemption in their lives. And the fruit tastes bad to people who are not part of the community. It yields some life, yes, but isn't this the soil in the body of Christ that is drying up? That has journeyed so far from being rich, diverse, enemy-loving, hospitable, sustainable, life-giving soil that it no longer innovates, relates, welcomes, or leads. It is rooted in self-centered production, not Christ.

It's not supposed to be this way. As Eugene Peterson wrote so gloriously in *The Message* paraphrase of the Bible,

All this energy issues from Christ: God raised him from death and set him on a throne in deep heaven, in charge of running the universe, everything from galaxies to governments, no name and no power exempt from his rule. And not just for the time being, but forever. He is in charge of it all, has the final word on everything. At the center of all this, Christ rules the church. The church, you see, is not peripheral to the world; the world is peripheral to the church. The church is Christ's body, in which he speaks and acts, by which he fills everything with his presence. (Eph. 1:20–23)

What a holy vision! A people with Christ Jesus at the center. This is the authority love gives. This is the power of rest and joy, salvation and repentance, connection and community. We are the people by which Christ speaks and acts. What are we saying to the world? How are we acting? We are the people by which he fills everything with his presence. In his presence there is fullness of joy, there is peace, there is heavenly strategy, there is the goodness and grace of God, there is room for each of us. Not a monoculture but a rich realm of diversity and possibility, the representation of every nation on the earth.

If all of this seems dead to you in the church, then I have good news: God is reviving us.

There is a painful history between Christians and creation. Since the days of Cain and Abel, blood cries out from the ground, and as Romans 8 tells us, the whole of creation is (and has been) groaning together. We sense that, do we not? The whole earth aching for renewal, hungry for human flourishing. Go with me on an agricultural journey of death and revitalization. This wisdom is a lamp unto our feet, life into our bones, as we walk on dry land, thirsty for living water.

Monocropping in America began in the early 1900s during the second Industrial Revolution, with the rise of the textile, coal, iron, and railroad industries and the expansion of electricity, petroleum, and steel. Not only did the end of slavery (and the beginning of Jim Crow's brutal segregation) mean a labor loss to many White landowning men, but new machinery and the beginning of commercial farming also meant the opportunity to produce a higher yield at a lower cost. Never mind the devastating loss of vital nutrients in the soil, the contamination of water in communities from the pesticides now required to help a farm flourish (without the help of natural elements as in a more diverse farm), and the impact on smaller farms as well as farm workers both here and in South America who were also pressed to produce more.

Economist and author John Ikerd, in his critique of these practices, said, "We bent nature to serve our needs. We achieved the economies of large-scale, specialized production as we applied the principles, strategies, and technologies of industrialization to farming."[2] The underbelly of our free-market economy is that companies make decisions for the bottom-line dollar, falsely building as though the ends justify the means.

Ray Bradbury wrote in *The Illustrated Man*, "Too much of anything isn't good for anyone."[3] When one crop dominates the soil, creation is at risk for famine and death, both the ground and the humans who live upon it. When one culture dominates the church, the heartbeat is faint and there is a death to diversity, the very thing that brings new life. As the nation goes, so the church goes, and many of us know the sting of feeling chewed up and spit out by our local churches. Perhaps you know how it feels for your spiritual leaders to use your labor, talent, and ideas to build their agenda. It's painful and the healing journey is long. But the ends do not justify the means in any industry, especially the church.

Similarly, due to monocropping, not only is our soil suffering but for decades farm workers had no rights. Many men and women held up the entire agriculture industry for very little pay, and with terrible treatment, while very few at the top of the leadership structure benefited financially and corporately. The bottom-line dollar drove decisions, again, with little focus on the means toward that financial end. It took the establishment of the National Farm Workers Association and United Farm Workers, founded by Cesar Chavez and Dolores Huerta in the early 1960s, for farm workers to gain the right to organize in order to bargain for better pay and better working conditions. Even under the threat of violence, arrest, and persecution, these farm workers have led the charge toward a more humane right to work and live in America.

Along with its historically poor treatment of farm workers and immigrants, commercial farming also uses pesticides and synthetic fertilizers that are wreaking havoc on the land we need to continue to feed our nation and our animals, which are also feeding our nation. Agriculture runoff pollutes ground and surface waters, degrading aquatic life and poisoning water in communities.

This same mindset was on display during the recent Flint, Michigan, water crisis. As companies along the Flint River disposed of waste and pollutants into the soil and water, children and families required to drink its water suffered from both environmental injustice and systemic racism. Murderous problems such as lead poisoning, skin rashes, hair loss, pneumonia, and more ravaged bodies, robbing children and adults of their capacity to focus and flourish in life. People have been required to spend time boiling water for baths, meals, and bottles, and engage in forced advocacy with city leaders and landlords, all while trying to work and live their lives. Not to mention the higher expenses of doctors' bills and the cost of fixing corroded pipes in homes.[4]

Globally, we use three million tons of pesticides per year, affecting human health and poisoning both water and land, thereby increasing the risk of cancer and causing long-term effects on the immune, reproductive, and nervous systems. The social costs of this kind of farming include the deterioration of rural communities as smaller farms shut down, which leads to less community support for local institutions such as churches, retail businesses, and schools. This has a critical effect on quality-of-life issues.[5] The number of farms continues to decrease annually even as the acres used for farming continue to increase, demonstrating again the focus on production and consumption instead of sustainability and health for farmers and farm workers and the community at large. Spiritually speaking, is this focus on high production, this reproducing of the same thing across the church, also costing us local microcommunities that cannot compete with megachurch ideals? Is the richness of our spiritual soil being eaten alive by monoculture?

———

Proverbs 13:23 says, "Much food is in the fallow ground of the poor, and for lack of justice there is waste" (NKJV). The first time I read that verse was in 2004, and it felt like the words and letters were lifting off the page. Has that ever happened to you? Where something just makes sense? Immediately, a picture of potential as a seed planted but never seen, never cultivated came into my mind. *For lack of justice there is waste.* The soil a seed grows in determines its foundation. The environmental factors, from diversity to nourishment to clean water to tilling, planting, and reaping. The right plant needs to be in the right soil. A weeping willow will not thrive in the desert. A cactus won't thrive in a swamp.

The same is true for humans. We do not choose the soil we are born into—our parents and their economics—nor do we choose the levels of abuse, neglect, or nurture; the access to health care and good education; or the shame or freedom we experienced. What happens when a child is unable to be nourished the way a parent might hope, due to environmental factors? When childcare is unaffordable and family caregivers are hurtful or harmful? When developmental milestones are missed due to lack of health care or lack of access to healthy foods? When parents are stressed about finances and bills and the potential for abuse or neglect increases? When caretakers do not have community or resources to help them parent, navigate transitions, or deal with difficult seasons of life? When the church focuses on production and misses the pain of the people? The soil is not cultivated—it lies fallow. *For lack of justice there is waste.*

Is this why some young people struggle to graduate from college? Is this how 145 million people in America remain at or below the poverty line for most of their lives? Are brilliant children with unique needs at home and at school overlooked, ignored, or assumed to be not smart because they do not have the support they need to flourish? Is this how people in faith communities, jobs, and schools are not valued or invited to offer their input and contribution because they don't fit the dominant narrative of expectations and appearance? What are we missing as a society and culture because we have one way, one particular standard of being in our world, and millions of people just do not fit that?

I believe what is happening in the natural realm of agriculture mirrors what is happening spiritually in America. In the 1900s and into the 2000s, institutions such as schools, universities, news, radio, television, businesses, churches, and more were dominated by White, male culture. Caucasian men held the narrative and set the tone for journalism, history, the selection of books and resources used to teach children and young adults in schools and churches, what was newsworthy and why it was so, what ads and marketing went to consumers, how women and minorities were portrayed, and so much more. This monoculture dominates the landscape of our nation's organizations and institutions. Of course, there are exceptions to this, but overall, there is one dominant ethos that paces our connections, education, and understanding. It's why many of us grow up learning that pilgrims and "Indians" were buddies at Thanksgiving. It's why we don't learn about the true horror of slavery, unless we were blessed to have a Black teacher, or a teacher committed to telling the whole truth, during the year that lesson is taught. It's why we don't understand class in America, or the intersections and impact of class, gender, and race. And so much more.

White men hold every major seat of power in the bedrock of our nation. White men dominate the top executive leadership position in *Fortune* 500 companies, which is another arena where they hold money and power; women comprise only 6 percent, or twenty-two, of the CEOs in these companies, making up 8 percent of top earners. Less than 2 percent of Latinx men are top earners, and only six Black men and eight men of Asian descent made the list. The wage gap between men and women, in this zone, is 18 percent, and CEOs typically earn $774 for every $1 their employees working minimum wage earn (women make up 50 percent of that group earning the lowest wage), and they earn $334 to every $1 against other salaries in their company.[6] And that's just one sector of the economy, to say nothing of education, media and entertainment, clergy, health care, and more. *For lack of justice there is waste.*

Churches are also dominated by one culture. Ordinary faithful believers are charged with building a "church" that only satisfies a singular, non-expansive vision of what the church should look like. And it is not only the popular face of evangelicalism as "America's religion" that erases the movement and mission in Black, Asian, and Latinx churches, but the publishing industry also allows one sound, one style, one culture to monopolize the industry and the public witness of worship songs, books, and other resources written by mostly Caucasian people. This is the reason many churches sing the same songs, preach the same teaching series, invite the same guest speakers to every conference, and avoid difficult issues and participation in the wider community outside of some holiday events. As Martin Luther King Jr. famously said,

> I think it is one of the tragedies of our nation, one of the shameful tragedies, that eleven o'clock on Sunday morning is one of the most segregated hours, if not the most segregated hours, in Christian America. I definitely think the Christian church should be integrated, and any church that stands against integration and that has a segregated body is standing against the spirit and the teachings of Jesus Christ, and it fails to be a true witness. But this is something that the church will have to do itself. I don't think church integration will come through legal processes. I might say that my church is not a segregating church. It's segregated but not segregating. It would welcome white members.[7]

For lack of justice there is waste.

In the same way that monocropping in agriculture has led to the death of farms and crops, I believe there is a connection spiritually between the one culture narrative and decline in church attendance,[8] as well as the death of the evangelical witness. Monoculture kills. The formulaic, mass production of Christianity is not God's highest and best for communities of people. Diversity, the habitual practice of gathering with people who don't look like, think like, or vote like us, and including even our enemies, is the way forward because it creates and sustains life.

Remember *The Biggest Little Farm*? We see that when all creation is allowed to live, contribute, and be itself, the whole thing flourishes. The same is true for communities of people. Where there is life-giving opportunity, absence of power dynamics that lead to competition and control, and a safe culture with healthy boundaries, people grow together. They flourish. They change. They learn to love differences, and even their enemy, as Jesus instructs. A community like this is compelling and sustainable.

Perhaps ironically, sustainability and health are the reasons given by most churches that decide not to pursue true diversity. Diversity takes so much time, an almost unbearable amount. That time grates against the allure of numbers that make the dominant group feel good: salvations, attendance, percentages of ethnic representation, giving, and so forth. But those numbers are unable to measure discipleship, equity in ethnic representation, or diversity of worship ethos, preaching (down to the sources used to prepare messages), and leadership. Not to mention the fact that really reaching different groups of people across race and class may decrease monetary giving even while health and vitality increase.

———

Mass production in American farming looked incredible—for about a hundred years. But now the monocropping farms are dying, and new life must be born. American churches have looked good for a long time too, but now the predominantly White churches and multicultural churches that are still White in method and mission are rapidly declining. Why are we holding on to the old way? Again, there is good news: churches all over the earth are exploding. What we call "minority churches" here—Asian, Latinx, and African—are growing, not shrinking. I'm not making a case that any of these churches are more holy than the others—rates of abuse, oppression and suppression of women, power struggles, and more are typically the same across the board in churches, no matter their denomination or ethnic makeup. I am simply stating that when one culture dominates over time, this produces death, not life.

So much of that faithful witness to Christ in other cultures is what the White church has tried to suppress, ignore, change, or erase, yet it is also the very nutrient their soil needs to not only grow their churches but sustain them. Many churches without a strong Caucasian presence choose a key focus on justice, suffering, and being a responsible presence in communities where their churches are planted, while many White churches have avoided justice (but not politics), tried to cheer people into victory rather than engage with suffering, and focused more on getting butts in seats than activating people to be like Christ in their communities. White people in churches are often taught a secular versus sacred narrative and set up their lives to avoid what they believe is bad and build what they believe is good. Many also cultivate an unhealthy separation from things they do not understand and spend more time judging "the world" than they do loving it.

Even though I was not raised this way, I have great sympathy for people who are born into things they cannot control. Again, we do not choose our soil. This can also be true for those of us with extremely broken backgrounds who enter churches looking for family and are naïve to how a church's teaching can impact our beliefs about the world. In a sense, we are reborn in our faith communities. We learn love, connection, and belonging as we participate and integrate into the common practices of the church we choose. For some of us, this produces recovery, restoration, reciprocity, and the capacity to work through hurts and offenses. But for others, this can mean an indoctrination of sorts where family members are cut off and the through line of legalism produces judgment, a sense of superiority or inferiority, and even a lurking, subtle hatred. Suddenly, despite having had no personal experience with a people group or issue, we can believe that God hates or wants to reform "the gays," that the legality of abortion alone should drive our political decisions, that immigrants are a problem in America, that we should guard the faith with territorial ministry and an "us vs. them" ideology. Often in communities like this, *unity* is actually a code word for assimilation.

But look at God—he will grow what he wants to grow, with or without our participation. The church is not dead. It is very much alive, and our love of Jesus is unbound by a building, denomination, or particular culture. If there is any blessing in the digital age, it's that we are exposed to diversity and deeply affected by the advocacy for greater representation of who we are as humans across every sector of society. (Though I must admit how sick I am of influencers and preachers who want to be my guru. There's always a weakness with every strength.) The decline in church attendance here in America, and frankly seminary and college enrollment too, is evidence that we are in desperate need of change. If American Christians desire to be first, to be the best, to lead the world—well, what we've become is arrogant, irrelevant, and unpersuasive.

In Matthew 20, Jesus says,

> You know that the rulers of the Gentiles lord it over them, and their high officials exercise authority over them. Not so with you. Instead, whoever wants to become great among you must be your servant, and whoever wants to be first must be your slave—just as the Son of Man did not come to be served, but to serve, and to give his life as a ransom for many. (vv. 25–28)

Not so with you. Our model is not the world we live in; it's Christ Jesus. The church is *us*, and while I will die on the hill of gathering for weekly worship, I will not die on the hill of a methodology that is a self-serving production spectacle that centers dominant culture and not the people it is called to shepherd. And I mean all people. The ones who don't look the way we think they should. The ones we reject because of their citizenship or nationality, their political beliefs or personal values. Jesus loves us all, and don't we each have enough sin and brokenness in our own lives that we can stop pointing fingers?

I've found the more I let Jesus deal with me, the less I feel compelled to deal with others. Just love the humans, or at least leave them alone. God is big enough to love and correct his kids, and he'll do it better than we will. Trust.

I'm encouraged to see that many are returning to the way of Jesus, even if we have been slow to do so. There is a need for us to examine who holds the dominant narrative in our faith communities. Who is missing? Why? How can we better cultivate the fallow ground of the poor? What is being wasted because of a lack of justice? We can recognize our tendency toward monoculture and begin the slow, arduous, messy work of spiritual biodiversity and polyculture. It is time for the church to be a place where people can grow, not in boxes we've created and assigned them to but the way God intends, so that our soil is rich, fertile, and full of life.

ATTITUDE: The more I diversify my life, relationships, and experiences, the more I will grow in humility and understanding.

AFFIRMATION: God loves diversity. He doesn't mind the mess, the chaos in real community, or the pace it takes to achieve optimal health. When I slow down, I am acting like Christ. When I love and welcome all people, my heart belongs to the Lord.

REFLECTION: Is it possible that my life is more monoculture than polyculture? Do I resist a diverse life and community because of my faith?

TECHNIQUE: Identify areas of hurry. Examine where outcomes and achievements, goals, and dreams overshadow health and community. What would it take to renew a right focus?

CHAPTER 9

When Conflict Calls

When you produce much fruit, you are my true disciples.
This brings great glory to my Father.

Jesus (John 15:8 NLT)

For thirty years, the Dominican Republic was controlled by a totalitarian dictator, Rafael Trujillo. Evil and petty, he employed secret police and controlled the nation's radio, press, mail, passport office, and even the airlines. Despite his work to build an elevated infrastructure for the Dominican people, the economic oppression and personal kickbacks he and his family received, as well as his heinous human rights violations, overshadowed his legacy. He tracked and murdered voices of dissent, and his obsession with women, particularly young girls, to whom he sent his military to coerce, force, or kidnap into his submission or to appear at his parties, led to the rape and abuse of women.

Born into a working-class family in San Cristobal, as the third of eleven children, this future "president" received little education and worked regular jobs. After joining the Constabulary Guard and rising through the military ranks, Trujillo was eventually named commander in chief of the National Army in 1927. And do you know who trained him?

We did.

During the US occupation of the Dominican Republic from 1916 to 1924, due to the American government's fear that Nazi Germany would take a stronghold to harm us within our own borders, the US military assisted in creating the Dominican Constabulary Guard, laying the foundation for both their National Guard and what is known today as the Dominican National Police. During this time, Trujillo was trained by the US Marines before becoming commander in chief.

Through a political alliance, violent elimination of enemies, and a rigged election in 1930, Trujillo then became president. Throughout his thirty years as a dictator, many resistance movements grew underground, including that of the Mirabal sisters. Forced to attend one of his parties, the sisters—Minerva, Patria, María Teresa, and Dedé—soon realized that Minerva was his target. The young women were faithful Catholics, married to good men they loved, and law-abiding citizens. When Minerva refused his sexual advances at the party, Trujillo not only took her on as a sexual conquest but made her life a living hell. She was studying at law school, and he had her banned from classes. He imprisoned her father, who was brutally tortured and died soon after being released. He held her and her mother hostage at a hotel, her only hope of release dependent on her sleeping with him. She refused again, and they escaped, but the harassment continued.

The Mirabals' finances were ruined, and the government began to monitor every move they made. Three of the four sisters responded by becoming activists. At the kitchen table where they also fed their children, the families gathered to craft makeshift bombs out of firecrackers. Known by their code name, Las Mariposas, the three sisters and their husbands were jailed for an assassination attempt, but the women were quickly released due to international pressure. Trujillo's international relationships had begun to fall apart after he unsuccessfully tried to murder the president of Venezuela.

The husbands were transferred to a remote jail nestled in the mountains, and the Mirabal sisters met death on their way to visit them. Trujillo's secret police strangled and beat the three women to death, then shoved their bodies back into their vehicle and pushed the car over the cliff to make it look like an accident. In spite of overwhelming evidence of their murder, there was no justice in the legal system; but the deaths of these mothers, wives, Christians, and community organizers in 1960 served as a catalyst for the end of the era of Trujillo. Something about watching women die at the hands of a brutal dictatorship became more than the Dominican people could bear.

Six months later, on May 30, 1961, a group of seven assassins, some who were actively involved in the president's military, successfully killed Trujillo in a gun battle as he traveled from the capital to his hometown of San Cristobal, where he was purportedly seeing his mistress.

Dedé, the sister who'd remained less active in the resistance, raised her sisters' sons and daughters, several of whom went on to serve in the future government of the Dominican Republic. And on February 7, 2000, the United Nations chose November 25, the day of the death of the Mirabal sisters, as the International Day for the Elimination of Violence Against Women.[1] The crushing loss of Las Mariposas serves as a reminder that ordinary people can make an extraordinary difference.

———

I highly doubt that Minerva dreamed of becoming an object of sexual desire for the most powerful man in her nation. I'm sure she never imagined her father would be imprisoned and tortured over her courage to say no. Who in the world plans to sit at the same table where children are fed making bombs and plotting the death of an evil leader? I imagine her aspirations as a wife and mother included integrity and deep commitment to her faith but did not include separation from her husband and brutal strangulation by a dictator's henchmen.

The conflicts we face are not always imaginable, predictable, or comfortable.

When the economic crisis since labeled the "Great Recession" struck, nearly ten million Americans lost their homes between 2006 and 2014. Today, 47 percent of people in America rent their homes, a figure that has more than doubled from 21 percent in 2006. Median home prices are up 50 percent since their lowest value during the recession, and home affordability is at an all-time low. In addition, student debt has doubled. Although studies estimate six million more Americans can afford a mortgage, and in some cases rent is equal to or higher than owning a home, the current loan process will not allow people to proceed with purchasing.[2]

The *LA Times* reported that shortly following the bankruptcy filing of the Lehman Brothers investment bank, on September 15, 2008, "Nearly 9 million people lost their jobs and at least 10 million lost their homes. Within four years, 46.5 million Americans were living in poverty."[3] Despite the crash, the rebound's effect of doubling housing costs, and rents skyrocketing all over America, the US government has not passed a bill raising the federal minimum wage since 2007. That's the year they agreed one dollar an hour more was plenty for working Americans, and $7.25 remains the minimum wage per hour for workers.

Losing a home, entering—or reentering—poverty, struggling to make ends meet, and making peace with potentially never owning property or land introduces people to the unpredictable and daily tension of financial insecurity. Like an ocean eroding rocks, this level of widespread suffering erodes trust. Society shifts toward unrest. Fear is the air we breathe, and without a disruption, we struggle to return to love.

The current housing crisis is one small example in a long history of stressful events and systems in need of an overhaul. For those who walk with Jesus, what matters most is who we become in the process. What is our response to injustice, systems we cannot control, economic failure, and other unpleasant surprises in our personal lives?

From her response to Trujillo, it's clear that Minerva had been growing that fruit of resistance and sowing integrity into her character. She was faithfully committed to her husband, family, and community and was in control of her emotions, her body, and her mind. She didn't give in, and she didn't give up. She was steadfast until the end.

What are you growing? When no one is watching, what are your faithful ordinary practices? Will they sustain you when conflict calls?

Because sometimes we are just living our lives, and then a doctor's diagnosis threatens our life or the life of someone we love. A habit to take the edge off every now and again turns into a full-blown addiction. We didn't see the affair or the divorce coming. One of our children drops a bomb on us about their experience or belief system. We suffer a loss so devastating that we don't know how to move forward. A mistake we've made destroys our reputation, income, or family. Life becomes so monotonous that we are numb and perpetually disappointed.

These are the moments we discover what we're made of, what's living inside of us. And you know what? You have permission to have no idea what to do next. If you cannot get out of bed for days, it is what it is. Anger, grief, rage, sorrow—these are correct responses to pain, not responses to correct. There is a time to get off the floor, and it is usually not immediately. You are loved. You are held by a God in heaven who loves you. Saint Hildegard said, "God hugs you. You are encircled by the arms of the mystery of God."[4]

Certainty is not our portion. Difficult and unfamiliar times require us to lean into the mystery of God. Life is a radical teacher, and one of its main lessons is how little control we have over anything. What do we do with our tension? Our uncertainty? How do we respond to the conflicts in our lives?

———

Conflict is unavoidable. Unlike the Mirabal sisters, most of us will probably not be called to topple a dictatorship. But we will have to face ourselves, deal with the tension in our lives, and choose to engage in uncomfortable situations and conversations. Our integrity and convictions will be tested in our home, workplace, friendships, and faith communities. Oh, and on Facebook as well. God help us over there.

Many people falsely believe that every tension must be resolved before we can move forward in a relationship, and if resolution does not seem possible, it feels easier to stay silent, gossip about the situation, or use our words in a way that tears the other person down rather than working toward resolution. We are hesitant to face the immediate pain that comes from engaging in a conflict because we do not keep the end goal of intimacy and connection in mind. As James Baldwin said, "Not everything that is faced can be changed, but nothing can be changed until it is faced."[5] Amen.

Now, here's how to engage in conflict in a way that will lead to health and more thriving relationships. I've put a special note at the end of this section for those of you who are reading this and are in an unhealthy or even unsafe or abusive relationship that you don't know how to navigate. Please know that these steps might be helpful to you in some of your relationships, but more is required in those situations where we are in danger or are being harmed. You are not alone.

Make conflict normal.

The first step is acknowledging that confrontation is part of every relationship. When people go to the gym, resistance is what builds strength. It's the same in real life—tension helps us grow. Without resistance bearing down on us, we'll have no opportunity to practice patience, honesty, and listening during a conflict. Like it or not, conflict is here to stay.

Understand "fight, flight, or freeze."

Most of us have a knee-jerk response to confrontation—fight, flight, or freeze. Fighters tend to respond quickly in the moment. Their level of emotional and mental health determines how aggressive that response is. Flight folks flee conflict immediately, and again, their level of health determines the degree. People with the freeze response may look like a deer in headlights, but usually what happens, and why this is potentially the most dangerous response, is they do not literally freeze but rather go through the motions. They may seem to be a high-functioning person, say the "right thing" or compromise, or do what is considered "appropriate," but inside they are disconnected and shutting down. This might be why suddenly a marriage ends or a relationship goes away. Freeze responders tend to struggle to express emotions and share honestly about the internal and external realities they face.

Good news for us: we might have a particular leaning, but we're all a combination of all three of these responses. Any given situation can pull any of them from us.

Pray before reacting.

Okay, look, I hate when people say this, but it's important. I am going to come at this from a different angle, because I think the whole "respond instead of react" messaging in churches is actually a way for people to avoid or control difficult emotions and conversations. Anger is sometimes the right response. Saying ouch is the right response when something hurts. Silence can be a good response, especially for internal processors who need more time to think. So, when I say pray before reacting, I do not mean for you to make sure your response is perfect enough to please every person in your life before you give it. I mean: *Help me, Jesus, please and thank you.* A simple prayer that sets the tone for engagement is a wise start to every conflict.

Ask for help.

Why do we think we need to do everything alone? It is okay to need help! Asking for help is normal—it does not make you weak; it makes you strong. If your boss is completely unreasonable, you will need help confronting them about their behavior. If you are struggling to communicate in your marriage, you will need help to engage with your partner. If you've never parented a teenager, why in the world would you know how to deal with the tension you're facing for the first time? If your family member is acting a fool, you will likely need tips on how to stay calm or not shut down during a confrontation. Ask for help! A trusted friend, a wise elder, a person who's been there—ask for specific wisdom for your situation and heed it.

Ask yourself some questions.

A question I ask myself (and God): *Is this about me and what I want, or is this about something that's important for this relationship to grow?* Other good questions to ask:

- Is there a log in my eye? (Matt. 7:3–5)
- Am I mad that I'm not getting my way?
- Is this just a different way? (Because my way is not *the* way, and a different way isn't a *bad* way.)
- What's my motivation? Why?
- Is this really about that, or is something deeper going on in me?
- What are my triggers (the things that tend to easily set me off)?

Use I-statements and no cross talk.

When pursuing healthy conflict, recovery work is a gift, and there are a few principles we need to stick by to create an atmosphere free from blame, shame, advising, and fixing. First, we start our shares with "I," not with "you." For example, "When you said this, it made me feel like this. Is that what you intended?" or "When you did this, it made me feel like this. Can you see how that was hurtful?" Immediately, this causes us to switch from blaming the other person for our emotions to taking responsibility for our emotions. We're also inviting the other person to share their intentions or reasons behind what they did or said. At the end of the other person's share or perspective, a great question our marriage mentors taught us to ask is, "Is there more?" And then we mirror the response. "What I hear you saying is this. Do I have that correct?" It creates a healthier dialogue.

Second, we follow the no cross talk principle. Cross talk is when you talk over someone as they share, or offer them tips and ideas, or begin to talk about yourself. Nope, none of that belongs in a conflict. There's no interrupting, just active listening. We're not there to fix, advise, or save but to listen, dialogue, and connect. If we have some advice we want to give, instead of offering it unsolicited, we can ask, "Can I share with you something that really helped me when I went through something similar?" Or "Would you like me to just listen, or do you need help with solutions?" Nothing shuts a person down like all your advice precisely nobody asked for.

Avoid always and never.

You always . . . You never . . . First of all, no, they don't *always* or *never* do anything. Even a broken clock is right twice a day. Second, these words turn a conflict about one issue into a conflict about never getting it right or always getting it wrong, and not about the original issue. Shaming each other will not resolve the real issue, nor will it lead to a healthy dialogue.

Know the goal.

Fighting just to fight is frustrating. Ten out of ten do not recommend because it resolves precisely *nothing*. What is the goal of the conflict? To establish understanding? To be heard? To find a compromise or solution? To communicate a hard truth? To end a relationship or change its boundaries? These are all incredible goals, but you have to know what you're working toward. Establish that on the front end. You can say something like, "My goal in this conversation that will probably be tough for us is this. Is there anything you'd like to add?" And then do something tough: stick to that. One problem at a time is better than ten problems at once. And speaking of that . . .

Stick to the original issue.

Have you ever been in an argument about something and all of a sudden the other person brings up what you did on February 4, 1996, and November 10, 2003, and also has a list of other unaddressed problems? This usually results in either a knockdown, drag-out fight or a complete shutdown. Whenever we feel terrible about ourselves, we'll struggle to manage conflict well. Such dredging can be a way for one person in the relationship to avoid acknowledging the hurt or harm they've caused. Instead of taking responsibility for their actions, they bring up issues from the past or other unresolved conflicts, which allows room for avoidance and shifting the blame. When this happens, redirect. "I know that was a really tough time in our relationship and it's important to talk about any unresolved hurt we may carry from that conflict. But right now, I think it's important for us to focus on the issue at hand, which is this." Stick to the original issue, one thing at a time.

Unspoken expectations are unfair expectations.

This is hard for some people. But you are grown. People do not exist to complete you, make you happy, please you, or meet all of your expectations. Also, you're not perfect. Nor do you exist to fix everything, make people happy, or meet all their expectations. So, the best we can do is to say we're sorry often. Own your mess. Hold other people accountable to own theirs. A good boundary knows where we end and another person begins. Ask yourself regularly, *What's my part? What are my unspoken expectations?* In general, expectations will make or break your life. This is especially true in conflict. Many conflicts are ongoing, because they are tensions to manage on a regular basis. Let go of the expectation you'll solve a problem every time you encounter one. Learn to be kind in tension, to still be yourself, to not wait on resolution to be in relationship.

Finally, here's a list of things to avoid completely.

- *Name-calling.* Stop trying to own the libs on Facebook—and seriously, in real life, do not resort to name-calling. It's unhelpful and hurtful. In long-term relationships, that stuff sticks and creates a habit that is hard to break. Stop doing it, and don't let people do it to you. "I don't appreciate you speaking to me like that, and I am going to walk away from you until you are calm enough to have this conversation without calling me names." Or sometimes, maybe you say, "Were you raised in a barn? Have you lost your mind talking to me like that? You picked the right one today!" Because nobody's perfect, remember?

- *Cursing.* While I know this isn't true for a lot of Christians, I personally am not hung up on actual cuss words. So here's what I mean: don't cuss at people in a conflict. If you want to use certain words as adjectives to express strong emotions sometimes, fine; but do not cuss straight at the humans. It will likely escalate the conflict, so take a deep breath (or a break if needed), calm down, and choose other words.

- *Threatening abandonment.* "I will divorce you, leave you, quit this or that, hurt or harm myself, if you do or do not do this." This level of manipulation and control is absolutely unacceptable. Do not do it, and do not accept it.

- *Abuse of any kind.* Verbal, physical, emotional, and spiritual abuse or neglect are all dangerous to our personhood, self-esteem, quality of life, and relationships. There is hope and there is help.

As I mentioned earlier, these steps are for people who are in mostly healthy or mildly dysfunctional relationships. For those of you who may be in a marriage, friendship, or working relationship that is toxic or abusive, these communication tools may serve as a guide but will likely not help you in the same way.

———

Where there is severe physical, sexual, emotional, or mental abuse or spiritual manipulation and control, additional help is required from a professional. As much as I believe in the idea of lay counseling within churches, it is insufficient in these situations. There is not enough emphasis on getting out and getting help. If your life is in danger, if your children's lives are in danger, step one is to get out. Professional help is needed immediately. The help of therapists, social workers, advocates, community organizers, clergy leaders, and even law enforcement when appropriate is necessary to stop the cycles of abuse. This is what professionals call "wraparound services." I like that term, because that is what this level of conflict takes: a community of professionals, advocates, witnesses, helpers, and healers to wrap around you if you take that huge step to leave.

Friend, this is not your fault. Even if you have made some mistakes, even if you played a part in enabling the abuser in your life, this is not your fault. You did not make someone abuse you. They chose to abuse you, and you can make the choice to leave. I remember the shame I carried after I was raped because I was drunk. I was completely convinced it was my fault. *If I hadn't been drunk this would never have happened*, I told myself. But I was wrong. An abuser knows how to see, manipulate, and exploit vulnerabilities. They take advantage of people they perceive to be weaker.

I want to tell you what I wish someone had told me: You are strong. I don't mean the kind of strength the world sells, where you have to fight, prove, and strive—maybe there's a time for that, but right now, you have the strength to walk away. In the notes section you'll find more information about hotlines and websites you can access that may help you take the first step.[6] And if you have a true trusted friend, tell them about your situation. If they tell you to stay, to give grace, to remain in an abusive situation, then they are not safe, and you should try someone else or go the third-party option for a professional who will know how to instruct you to get to safety. It's not supposed to be this way. I pray you receive all the help you need, and quickly.

———

When my husband and I work with people, especially couples or those facing difficult challenges at work, we offer the following suggested phrases to aid you as you strive for healthy conflict. I'm hoping they help you get honest, take time to process (in case you're an internal processor and the other person is an external processor), and respond in a way that facilitates healthy dialogue.

- I'd like to take a minute to process that.
- I'm feeling upset and a bit angry at the moment, and I'd like some time before we keep working together to resolve this issue. I am not walking away from you, but I want to use my words wisely, and I am not sure I can do that right now.
- I can tell you're feeling upset; how can I help us process this well?
- I don't think walking away right now is the right answer.
- I need a break.
- I don't think this is the best place for us to have this discussion—can I schedule some time with you in one of our offices later today?

- Before we get into this—I do want to have this conversation, but I am not at my best at ten o'clock at night and I want to be present to you. How about tomorrow, on our lunch breaks, we pick this up again?

As often as possible, learn to say what you think. Learn to ask for what you need. Learn to ask for help. That's responsible adulting, and we need more of it in our world.

———

Now let's talk about digital engagement. Some folks are just working out their real-life aggression on the interwebs, and it shows. But now that we've learned a little about conflict resolution with actual people, it's also important to know how to engage online with content and with others. The average American adult spends two hours a day on social media, with the most popular site being Facebook.[7] This is much more time than most people spend talking to a person per day.

First, think critically. Does the website end with .blogspot. gov.uc.sm.com.org? Probably not a real site. Where does the meme originate? Who is posting it, and why? Is that article an opinion piece? What are its sources? Who owns the website that published it? Who funds that organization? Think, think, think! If you are a human, much less a Christian, you are responsible for what you share, like, and repost. Be a good internet citizen, and *think*.

If you want to comment on a post, ask questions. "That's an interesting take—how did you arrive at that conclusion?" "Can you share more data about this situation?" Make suggestions about data, or offer thoughtful takes from a different perspective. It's okay to go back and forth sometimes, but don't argue, fight, or name-call. Those are nothing but a time suck for real.

Know when to go private and when to go public. If you have relational capital with someone, engage with them—send a text, go private in the direct messages, have a conversation. Recently, someone I care about posted a propaganda piece that was in the vein of causes she's passionate about. I direct messaged her and gently shared the source of the piece and what it meant. Folks were shaming her left and right in the comments for something she thought was a good thing—she didn't have a clue, and she deleted it immediately.

Sometimes it's good to stay public in the comments section. Just like we do in real life, people need an example of healthy engagement, especially healthy disagreement. I don't recommend writing, "This is hot trash." (Like I did on an evangelist's post after he made a video saying anyone who voted for Joe Biden was voting for the devil and was not a Christian. Not only is that unbiblical and also undemocratic, it is simply unacceptable.) On my better comment threads, there are many moments when someone then sends me a direct message thanking me for my engagement online, for standing up for a person or people group that was being attacked, or for calling out someone's racist, sexist, or rude behavior. Pray, asking God to help you discern when to speak and when to be silent, when to confront publicly and when to confront privately. Listen to the Prince of Peace. He will help you, and if you're unsure, take a beat. Think. Come back later if it still seems right to you.

Be a good listener online. What are people really saying? If I push past my judgment, I can often hear fear, anxiety, overspiritualizing, anger, frustration, or loneliness. What do you really hear? I'm not recommending you assign things to people—let's not go all Judge Judy here—but before you pop off, or before you create content to share, what do you hear? What do people need? What do you have to share that will help them with their deeper fear? That's my favorite thing about Jesus. He always listens beyond the words and the situation—he hears our felt need. How can we listen better, even online? It is possible for us to be a source of peace instead of an instigator of conflict. To pull people together more than we tear them apart.

I want you to know that there are incredible people and Christians out there doing the Lord's work. The fruit of the Holy Spirit is strong in them—they have a faithful witness unto Christ Jesus. Many people are gathering at home with family and friends, pursuing careers or degrees, showing up to work, and participating in our local communities and churches. And in that sacred, very ordinary life, there is evidence of the fruit of the Holy Spirit. People are practicing

- love when it would be easier to hate.
- joy when despair is the more logical response.
- peace in chaos and turmoil.
- patience in a hurried, me-first culture.
- kindness when annoyance and irritability come more naturally.
- goodness when apathy and numbness creep into our connections.
- gentleness when wrath and anger threaten to take over.
- faithfulness in a flaky, unfaithful, individual culture.
- self-control in a freedom-chasing, pleasure-seeking society.

Like the Mirabal sisters, when conflict calls, they are willing and ready, anchored in integrity, tested, tried, and true. They are loving and honest in their daily life and relationships, growing, changing, and cultivating peace. This is who we are called to be in the beautiful and absolutely insane world that God entrusts to us.

ATTITUDE: Conflict is normal. There is nothing wrong with me.

AFFIRMATION: I am capable of handling confrontation, even if my track record or family of origin says i am not. I am growing in the skill of managing healthy conflict. My connections to others, and the intimacy in my relationships, are strengthened by engaging in healthy conflict.

REFLECTION: What is my regular response to conflict? Do I fight, take flight, or freeze? What about the Mirabal sisters moments of my life? Have I risen to the demand, or have I been crushed under the pressure? What would I do differently if I could?

TECHNIQUE: I gave you so many in this chapter. Go review!

CHAPTER 10

Woe to the Offender

I n 2006, Charles "Charlie" Roberts walked into the West Nickel Mines Amish schoolhouse near Lancaster, Pennsylvania, and opened fire. He killed five children, injured five more, and then committed suicide.

In 2015, an American terrorist and White supremacist named Dylann Roof hid a Glock 41 .45-caliber handgun on his person, walked into a prayer meeting at the historic Mother Emanuel Church in Charleston, South Carolina, and murdered nine people, including the senior pastor and a state senator. Roof confessed his intention was to start a race war and was sentenced to nine consecutive life sentences.

In 2017, Devin Patrick Kelley carried an assault rifle into First Baptist Church in Sutherland Springs, Texas, and committed the largest mass shooting in the state's history by murdering twenty-six people ranging in age from seventeen months old to seventy-seven years old. One family alone lost eight people that day. As Kelley was leaving the church, a local neighbor shot him twice, in the torso and leg, and Kelley then died due to a self-inflicted gunshot wound to the head.

In 2019, off-duty Dallas police officer Amber Guyger walked into the home of Botham Jean and shot and killed him. In a rare case of police accountability, Guyger was sentenced to ten years in prison for her unthinkable decision.

What is the through line in each of these tragedies? Forgiveness.

Without a whole lot of time passing, family members stood to publicly forgive the murderers in the aftermath of these killings. During victim testimonies, parents, siblings, and loved ones expressed their grief and offered forgiveness to Roof and Guyger. The Amish community wrapped its arms around the parents of Charlie Roberts. Church members chose to forgive Kelley for destroying the lives of twenty-six people and those they left behind.

———

Forgiveness is a powerful, life-changing experience. It is a healing agent in a world full of conflict, turmoil, and chaos. It is biblical to turn the other cheek, to love our enemies, to forgive over and over again. In Matthew 18:21–22, Peter, like the rest of us, has a question about forgiveness. "Then Peter came to Jesus and asked, 'Lord, how many times shall I forgive my brother or sister who sins against me? Up to seven times?' Jesus answered, 'I tell you, not seven times, but seventy-seven times.'" Because love always lands on the side of mercy. Even when it feels impossible, this is who we are as believers.

As a habitual practice, the giving and receiving of forgiveness helps us achieve greater liberation. No one owns our mind when we forgive. We are not a slave to an act that happened to us, or one we perpetuated, when we pursue forgiveness. It keeps the heart pure. I know this on a deep personal level. Forgiveness is a radical act of freedom.

Can I be honest, though? When it comes to certain acts of violence and injustice, I'm more like Jonah. His story in the

Bible is a wild one, and when I was little, it was a regular on the Sunday school rotation. What child isn't excited about a giant fish swallowing up a whole human and then spitting him out again once he gets his act together?

I'll tell you who: me. This sounds like when you are waiting around for punishment and then you get grounded from Nintendo, your pager, and your friends for three weeks. Also, this story is terrible. How is this real? Is anyone buying it? Doesn't it sound like a great bedtime story parents cooked up as they were writing parts of the Bible in the fourth or fifth century, when they wanted to scare the bejeezus out of their children? Obedience comes in the form of sheer terror in some Southern (and apparently also some Jewish) households.

So God tells Jonah to go on to Nineveh because he has some people there he wants to save. Other kids, even though they are bad kids. And Jonah starts side-eyeing God from jump and says, "What you say, Lord? Nineveh? Nineveh no. Nineveh *nevah*. You already know what they did to our people. Stop playing games; I'm heading out to Tarshish. I need me some Mediterranean Sea vibes because you, O Lord, have really stressed me out with these heathens killing and oppressing my people. They got big military and big money. They deserve everything coming to them, and I don't think they are worthy of salvation. So, if you want them saved, God? You do it yourself. I AIN'T GOING. I'll see you after my Tarshish vacation."

I picture God in this moment like my mama—and some of y'all's mamas—looking at me like, "Go on 'head, I wish you would." And none of us really understanding what's about to happen to us. Jonah gets on a boat, and before long, everything goes terribly wrong. All the men on the small ship start trying to figure out who done it. Who made God mad? Whoever it is, they better come clean and get off this boat. Jonah, with the deep sigh, says, "It's me. Throw me over." And they do, which is how he ends up still alive in the middle of the sea in the belly of a fish.

Jonah stays mad through this whole story, which I can appreciate, because it's honest; but after some time in the guts and gross stuff, he's like, "I'll do it, okay? I'll go tell these people to repent." The big whale spits him onto shore. Jonah was so frustrated, but when he encounters the ruthless killers of Nineveh, he basically throws more shade and side-eye and says a few sentences that start with REPENT. After he's finally obeyed God—albeit with an attitude—he goes and sits, fuming mad. He's so mad, he tells God that he could die. God's like, "Who are you to be mad?" (*I am me*, I bet Jonah thought. *I am me to be mad*.) And in a nutshell, God says, "I save who I want to save, and who are you to be mad about it?"

Turns out this Bible story of my youth was a whole wild, nearly unbearable tale about enemy love. How could God want these people saved? After all the harm they did? If this story was *The Hunger Games*, Nineveh would be the Capitol, stinking like roses, killing kids in arenas, and in general not giving a rip about anything but money and power. I get why Jonah told God to save them himself and why, after he finally obeyed God, he was still mad.

People coming to the saving knowledge of Jesus or learning the love and mercy of God after they've murdered someone we love is not exactly what I'd call justice. *Good for you! Glad you're going to heaven now! Sure was fun to skip my Mediterranean vacation to preach to you. But my people are still oppressed or dead. So what do I care?* Jonah is a difficult story that I believe is less about a man's obedience and more about the merciful heart of the Father God. Not only do we see that mercy in God's love for the Ninevites but also in his love for Jonah, whom he did not turn away, or scold, or abandon. Jonah never fixes his attitude, and God just stays close. What a wonder he is.

I'm in awe of the quick process of forgiveness in all the tragedies I mentioned above. I don't know if I could make that offering. Forgiving the unforgivable takes time for me. It's a process. But I suppose when it comes to necessary, difficult decisions, we make them first and mean them later.

At the trial of Amber Guyger, Botham's brother, Brandt, gave a moving victim's testimony. His sincerity in his statement, where he expressed forgiveness for her decision to shoot and kill Botham, moved America. Across the internet, a photo of him hugging Amber, accompanied by captions about Christianity and doing the right thing, went viral, and he was lifted up for this courageous act. He deserves that praise. His brother was murdered. In his own home. In the face of the unthinkable, he did the impossible. Brandt showed mercy. As did the Nickel Mines Amish, the members of First Baptist Church in Sutherland Springs, and the families of the Charleston Nine.

It's hard to explain my challenge with that viral response from Christians on social media. I believe the Bible. I am intimately acquainted with the power of forgiving abusers, and I am living in the freedom of not seeing life, people, and circumstances through the lens of what has been done to me or what I have done to others. So why did the public reaction bother me?

The best way I can sum it up is that I felt the ulterior motive. *This is the way to handle injustice*, the posts seemed to communicate. Not anger, not rage, not grief, not policy change, not criticism. The "right way" is forgiveness, offered immediately and absent of accountability.

It's not the act of extending forgiveness that bothers me, it's the perpetual persistence with which Christians urge people to calm down in the face of tragedy, oppression, and injustice. This gross insistence that God is pleased only when we obey perfectly and offer forgiveness quickly and freely. But the story of Jonah suggests that God accepts our painfully slow, stubborn obedience, and that he does not remove his presence when we can offer him only attitude and stank eye.

"God bless Botham Jean's brother," Bernice King, daughter of Martin Luther King Jr., wrote on Twitter. "But don't confuse his forgiveness with absolving this nation for its gross, bitter discrimination against Black people in a myriad of its systems and policies. Racism and White supremacist ideology can't be 'hugged out.'"[1]

Sometimes in Christian communities we want forgiveness (with a high focus on *other people* giving it, no matter what they have suffered) without accountability, without consequence. It is celebrated and prized. But I think God cares about the offended and the offender, and I think his grace toward Jonah teaches us that he knows this is seriously hard stuff. We preach forgiveness literally all the time, and it is the crux of our faith, but hear me when I tell you we need to do more teaching about the one who causes the offense.

In Luke 17, "Jesus said to his disciples: 'Things that cause people to stumble are bound to come, but *woe to anyone through whom they come*'" (v. 1, emphasis added).

In Matthew 18, he said, "If anyone causes one of these little ones—those who believe in me—to stumble, it would be better for them to have a large millstone hung around their neck and to be drowned in the depths of the sea. Woe to the world because of the things that cause people to stumble! Such things must come, but woe to the person through whom they come!" (vv. 6–7).

Woe to anyone through whom they come. I'm no biblical Greek expert, but when I looked this up in Strong's concordance, it's basically an interjection for grief or denunciation. And what Jesus says sends a chill down my spine. It's "better for them to have a large millstone hung around their neck and to be drowned in the depths of the sea" than to have caused his little ones to stumble?

Maybe that's why God doesn't want Jonah or me or you to be so worried about what God is going to do with abusers, murderers, oppressors, and liars. Because he's saying, with great grief and denunciation, that he will deal with them. At the same time, as a community, we need to do better about holding people accountable for their behavior. Why is it always on the one who has been offended to be the bigger person and forgive? Why is there not more emphasis on the offender, to whom God says WOE, you need to repent, change, make amends, and grow? Isn't this the exact reason abuse continues to flourish? Why power and greed drive the hierarchy of humanity? Why people cycle out of the church when they are fed up and used up? Why women are often stuck in relationships feeling like everything is their fault?

Woe to the offender. Dietrich Bonhoeffer wrote about cheap grace and costly grace in his book *The Cost of Discipleship*. He said this:

> Cheap grace is the preaching of forgiveness without requiring repentance, baptism without church discipline, Communion without confession, absolution without personal confession. Cheap grace is grace without discipleship, grace without the cross, grace without Jesus Christ, living and incarnate.
>
> Costly grace is the treasure hidden in the field; for the sake of it a man will go and sell all that he has. It is the pearl of great price to buy for which the merchant will sell all his goods. It is the kingly rule of Christ, for whose sake a man will pluck out the eye which causes him to stumble; it is the call of Jesus Christ at which the disciple leaves his nets and follows him.

Costly grace is the gospel which must be sought again and again, the gift which must be asked for, the door at which a man must knock.

Such grace is costly because it calls us to follow, and it is grace because it calls us to follow Jesus Christ. It is costly because it costs a man his life, and it is grace because it gives a man the only true life. . . . Costly grace is the Incarnation of God.[2]

Forgiveness is the way of Jesus, and we are empowered to forgive because he has forgiven us. Forgiveness can be freely given. But you know what? It doesn't heal everything. Just like Bernice King said. Forgiveness does not absolve anyone from the need to change and to make what is wrong right. *Reconciliation* has become a buzzword in the church in recent years, particularly around the issue of race. Or, in denominations like the Southern Baptist Convention, reconciliation over sexual abuse in churches. All of a sudden, there were panels and interviews, sermon series, nights, conferences, and workshops on reconciliation. Rarely did we hear staff or leadership teams honestly say, when forgiveness came up, "We are the offender, and God takes this seriously. Better that we die in the sea like we were given a pair of cement shoes by a mafia member than wound the ones God loves. We're sorry. We take responsibility. We will make amends, and we will make this right."

As far as I can see, the focus continues to remain on the offended to forgive rather than on the offender to do better. As a victim myself, I still believe in this process—forgiveness absolutely does set us free. With or without the other person's participation, or ever hearing them say they're sorry, we can find freedom through forgiveness. Yes, and amen to that. C. S. Lewis said, "To be a Christian means to forgive the inexcusable because God has forgiven the inexcusable in you."[3] We all are in need of forgiveness, and the grace of God gives us power to do it.

Forgiveness and reconciliation are not the same thing. We choose to forgive freely, but trust must be earned. As my friend Harmony Grillo, author of *Scars and Stilettos*, often says, "There can be no reconciliation without recovery." If there is no change, there is no way forward in the relationship. An apology doesn't mean anything without changed behavior. Period. Plenty of abusers and manipulators say they're sorry all the time. In workplaces and in churches, instead of changing their egotistical power trips, authority figures offer opportunities and promises for promotion. In marriages and romantic relationships, presents and promises replace authentic recovery and change. In institutions like schools or police departments, community organizations and nonprofits, a public apology is often presented without any systemic justice or structural change. In families, all kinds of abuse are covered with silence and shame and with the abuser's refusal to get help or do the necessary work to stop committing the offenses.

When it comes to the church, can you imagine if the leadership began to hold its people, especially men, accountable to the hurt and harm they've caused? If believers, particularly clergy, understood the difference between costly and cheap grace, there would likely be a significant decline in church hurt, and perhaps less church decline. Can you imagine how different and how healthy communities could be and become? What level of authority and confidence is possible when people are empowered in safety and strength? When they know they are human beings, made in the image of God, who do not deserve mistreatment? How freeing it is to hear, "I'm so sorry I hurt you. I'm committed to change. Here's how I am/we are making this right." Could there be a more equitable and just experience in a community of faith than this?

Jesus said, "Woe to the offender." We must stop skipping over this in our messages on forgiveness. Jesus cares when we hurt people, and teachers of the Word, shepherds, will be held to a higher standard.[4] This needs to be a warning to us that we must heed. God is merciful, and God is also just. He will keep us accountable to him, whether in this lifetime or the next, and believers must stop pretending we can escape the justice of God.

To be clear: if you've suffered a serious offense, this means you can trust that God is on your side. He is taking care of it, even if it feels like justice will never come. And maybe it won't on this side of heaven. That's true for me—and the person who raped me. But through a long process of forgiveness, I've grown to trust that no one escapes God. We will all meet Jesus face-to-face, and God keeps accurate records. He is the Ancient of Days, merciful and just.

God was tender toward Jonah's pain and offenses, and God was tender toward Jonah's offenders, the Ninevites. It makes no good sense to me, because I feel strongly about some people not making it to heaven, fam. But it is what it is. And it is who he is, and the process of becoming like Christ means we grow in his tenderness toward ourselves and others. And while God clearly chooses whoever he wants to be saved, regardless of our big feelings, he also says, "Woe to the offender." The burden is not on the people who are hurt to do all the growing, changing, and forgiving.

If you are a leader in your home, business, church, or government, in law enforcement, or in any other place, repent for using your power to hurt others. Repent. Stop asking people (implicitly or explicitly) to enable you or remain complicit in order to keep their jobs or uphold the image of your reputation. Repent. Stop asking people to forgive you and then refuse to make the necessary changes, so the hurt and harm only continue. Repent. Stop using your giftedness and charisma as an excuse for your poor behavior. Repent. Stop being racist, sexist, power hungry, or greedy. Repent. Own your character flaws. Make amends and change.

For those who are standing silently, watching abusers abuse, bosses manipulate, clergy leadership obsess over themselves, and people make the money funny, repent. The compassionate love of Jesus compels us to speak and act. We must not enable hurt and harm. Repent. Yes, the cost is more than you want to pay, but it is worth every penny. Repent. Own your part. Make amends and change.

For those who must always forgive without hearing an apology, without seeing change, thank you for not shrinking the cross. For being obedient to God even when your arms are crossed, when you are so mad you could die. We bless you in the unseen spaces of healing from hurt and harm. You are loved. You are held. El Roi, the God Who Sees, is your Father, Mother, and Friend.

> **ATTITUDE:** I am capable of causing significant hurt and harm to others. There is no condemnation in Christ, but I am ready to take responsibility for my actions and hold others accountable for theirs.
>
> **AFFIRMATION:** God is merciful and just. He sees it all. He loves people I hate. He saves who he wants to save. I can trust him.
>
> **REFLECTION:** Is there anyone I believe should not be saved? Is there anyone I need to forgive? How do I need to repent for the hurt and harm I may have caused?
>
> **TECHNIQUE:** Write a letter to an offender they will never read. Do not edit yourself, just let it flow. Share the hurt, harm, and/or abuse they've caused you. Explain the impact on your daily life. How could your life have looked different if they had

not offended you this way? Be completely honest with what you've lost. After you write this, sit with God. He is close to the brokenhearted. He is a very present help in time of need. Ask for his comfort and care to heal this wound over time. Ask God if there is any next step he is inviting you to take. Receive his love and grace to keep going.

CHAPTER 11

I'll Love You till the Cows Come Home

I will love you till the cows come home, from a trip to Mars through skies unknown in a rocket ship made of glass and stone." I swallow. "I will love you till the cows come home." Slowly, the lump in my throat started to sting the back of my eyes, with the yaks in the Cadillac, the sheep setting sail on a cruise ship . . . wolves, pigs . . . frogs riding past.[1]

Deep breaths. Eyes closed. *No, you will not break down during story time. You will not break down during story time.* Sea horses, shrimp, bass . . . "I will love you till the deer dance by."

I feel the whisper of the Holy Spirit at my back: *This is how I love you. Not now*, I shoo him. Geese flap down, and then the ants march in with birthday cake on their chins, and I know he loves me like the cows in their pen. The book ends, with love making them lie down again. "I will love you till the cows come home. Come home."

Music in my mind, the scent of hundred-year-old pews, and my little hands holding a weathered and black Baptist hymnal.

"Ye who are weary, come home. Earnestly, tenderly, Jesus is calling, calling, 'O sinner, come home.'"

I kiss my children, not a single song to sing that night, and head straight to my shower to sob. I sit, even though my pregnant belly makes every ligament ache. *I love you,* I hear the Holy Spirit say again, but I am still not ready to receive his care. Nursing my wounds, rehearsing the words, disoriented from an embarrassing, public conflict, I sit under the water and let it wash me.

Water is healing, cleansing our impurities, washing our wounds. When I am weary of the world, when I am hurting and unable to carry on, I come to the water. The Holy Spirit meets me there, at the end of myself, where there are no clever answers, no words left. I feel able to let my guard down in this quiet space where God is. Here is where I am more inclined to let the Lord love me. Water is the essence of baptism. Into the water I go, a death to all that is not like him. Out of the water, I rise with hope. *Lord, make me new.*

========

If love is the resistance, then it starts here, in the secret place with him, in this baptism that calls for true repentance—real change in the way of Jesus. We are like Saul, certain of our way though our mindsets are murderous and our hatred for others feels justified, and we are meeting the Lord for a turning. An about-face from defiance toward loving our brothers and sisters into the impossible love of God where each and every person is made in his image and worthy of our love, respect, and honor. In the secret place, in the sacred ordinary of taking showers, washing dishes, going grocery shopping, changing diapers, and studying Scriptures, the tenderness of the One who comforts his people, the One who has compassion on the afflicted, meets us. He shows us the path of life. It is a mystery, but we are never the same.

The days are difficult, the times urgent. We are in need of comfort, and we are indeed afflicted—the difficulty will not cease, nor will the urgency relent. In his presence is fullness of joy; at his right hand are pleasures evermore. If God is love, then joy is also resistance. Joy in the middle of uncertainty. Joy in the face of conflict and tension. Pleasure is a freedom found in the goodness of a God who knew the hell we would be born into, because he bore it himself. A babe in a tiny manger and a mother who sang her song of praise:

> Oh, how my soul praises the Lord.
>> How my spirit rejoices in God my Savior!
> For he took notice of his lowly servant girl,
>> and from now on all generations will call me blessed.
> For the Mighty One is holy,
>> and he has done great things for me.
> He shows mercy from generation to generation
>> to all who fear him.
> His mighty arm has done tremendous things!
>> He has scattered the proud and haughty ones.
> He has brought down princes from their thrones
>> and exalted the humble.
> He has filled the hungry with good things
>> and sent the rich away with empty hands.
> He has helped his servant Israel
>> and remembered to be merciful.
> For he made this promise to our ancestors,
>> to Abraham and his children forever. (Luke 1:46–55
>> NLT)

He knows what we need. He knows when we need to be emptied and when we need to be filled. When we are hungry for justice, thirsty for righteousness, he will fill us with good things. When we are full of the riches of this world, he will send us away empty. He will bring us down from our high horses and he will exalt us when we are humble. God, in his mercy, will help us. He knows what we need.

He made a promise to our ancestors. A covenant forever binding us to him and to each other. We turn to him to remember: we are never alone.

Come home, come home. I will love you till the cows come home.

Sparrows descended on our yard this week, pecking at grass, eating the yellow flowers off my succulents, slurping sugar water from the hummingbird feeder. Their brown, beautiful bodies perched on branches, the edges of my pots, the corner of the fountain that needs to be filled. I don't know why they came, other than as an abiding reminder of God's promise to me to provide. The sparrow is a symbol in creation of his steadfastness, his faithfulness, his desire for me to commit to him for life. In my midtwenties, I had a tattoo artist etch a sparrow onto my rib cage. *How much more so does the Lord care for me*, is what I wanted to remember when I stood in front of my mirror. I wanted to know it in my bones, for the very marrow of my being to be consistently moved to trust.

The birds in my yard do not appear concerned about their coming and going, their presence and place, their needs and desires. They just exist. Take up space. Graze. Dare I say, they delight. Is this what it means to trust?

Rowan Williams writes in his book *Meeting God in Paul*, "The one thing you know for certain about your tiresome, annoying, disobedient, disedifying fellow Christians is that God has welcomed them; that becomes your challenge."[2]

It's highly likely that you and I—me especially—find ourselves so challenged. We cannot imagine God welcoming the ones who hurt us, who are so different than us, the ones who make our tummies coil with frustration and anxiety. Like Jonah, we find it difficult to imagine God loving them.

But he does. He loves them till the cows come home.

———

When we are hurt, it is difficult to see others from God's perspective. And you know what? Maybe sometimes we don't need to, especially when there is abuse and/or our well-being is perpetually in danger. Again, getting out for our own survival and safety is more important in that moment than seeking to offer our abuser mercy or to understand them in Jesus's name. It is not our responsibility to fix others or make them stop their harmful behavior, even when they make us feel that way. That's a person who would rather project onto you than make the necessary changes to not be a controlling, manipulating person. Own your part for enabling their poor behavior and, friend, *leave*. Ask for help and go. If you do not have anyone to call, if there is no place to escape, please call one of the local or national hotlines. You deserve better. You are worth more.

This includes people on the internet who are disturbing your peace. If Aunt Pearl won't stop posting propaganda comments on your posts, June Bug texts you corrections every time you say something, or random Boy Bobby from high school is always calling you a social justice warrior or a liberal feminist Marxist—well, this ain't nothin' a little unfollow, unfriend, mute, or snooze for thirty days option can't fix. Cultivating digital echo chambers where everyone always agrees with you is not a great idea, but wasting energy on rude people who want to be right all the time? No, thank you.

Emotional bruises impair our judgment. We start to group people to cope. All men are cheats. All Black people are criminals. All White people living in trailers are trash. All immigrants are illegals. All conservatives are racist bigots. All progressives

167

are communist socialists. All marriages are miserable. I could go on for days—you fill in the blanks of your belief systems here. We develop ideas that hinder complexity, nuance, relationship, and love. Clearly, the collective matters, but if we start to think that all the people who look like those who have hurt us are the same, then we will struggle to cultivate critical thinking and equitable living.

Sometimes, I find the Bible ridiculously challenging concerning these matters. It seems the writers desperately want us to understand that the love of God pushes way past our firmest boundaries, far beyond our natural way of thinking. In his letter to the Romans, the apostle Paul wrote,

> Accept the one whose faith is weak, without quarreling over disputable matters. One person's faith allows them to eat anything, but another, whose faith is weak, eats only vegetables. The one who eats everything must not treat with contempt the one who does not, and the one who does not eat everything must not judge the one who does, for God has accepted them. Who are you to judge someone else's servant? To their own master, servants stand or fall. And they will stand, for the Lord is able to make them stand. (Rom. 14:1–4)

The point is, we all look at folks in our lives, especially other Christians, and think to ourselves, *Their faith is weak sauce. Look at all that stuff they do—they are too free! They don't believe the true gospel—weak faith!* Or, *Look at all those rules they keep—they are too strict! They don't believe the true gospel—weak faith!* But look again at what the Lord says: "To their own master, servants stand or fall. And they will stand, for the Lord is able to make them stand" (v. 4).

Aren't each of us doing our best as individuals and as communities with our finite minds to interpret the will of an infinite

God? To hear from the Spirit, to instruct each other, to read Scripture and apply it to our lives? Who among us is doing this perfectly? Who among us is right all the time? Who are we to judge someone else's servant? If we are doing the best we can unto Christ, even if we're wrong about some things (hint, hint: we are), isn't the Lord able to make us stand?

That level of kindness, grace, and mercy makes me uncomfortable. But it's a good reminder that my judgments, and your judgments, don't amount to anything with Jesus. He is the One before whom we all will stand or fall, and Paul gives us great assurance that the Lord intends for those who love him to stand.

Paul, formerly Saul, a man rescued from a life of legalism, judgment, and murder (literally; he killed people who did not agree with his sect of theological ideology), continued his letter with these words:

> One person considers one day more sacred than another; another considers every day alike. Each of them should be fully convinced in their own mind. Whoever regards one day as special does so to the Lord. Whoever eats meat does so to the Lord, for they give thanks to God; and whoever abstains does so to the Lord and gives thanks to God. For none of us lives for ourselves alone, and none of us dies for ourselves alone. If we live, we live for the Lord; and if we die, we die for the Lord. So, whether we live or die, we belong to the Lord. For this very reason, Christ died and returned to life so that he might be the Lord of both the dead and the living. You, then, why do you judge your brother or sister? Or why do you treat them with contempt? For we will all stand before God's judgment seat. It is written:
>
> > "'As surely as I live,' says the Lord,
> > 'every knee will bow before me;
> >   every tongue will acknowledge God.'"

So then, each of us will give an account of ourselves to God. (vv. 5–12)

We're not going to get to heaven and give an account of all the people we policed in our cities, in our churches, and on the internet. God is not going to applaud us for "really keeping the true gospel." Instead, we will each give an account of *ourselves* to God.

All of this is powerful to read, digest, and apply, but what Paul said next really gets me. He gives us instructions on how our faith should affect others and how we are to steward our relationships—and not just the ones we really enjoy but also the ones that are a source of tension and disagreement.

> Therefore let us stop passing judgment on one another. Instead, make up your mind not to put any stumbling block or obstacle in the way of a brother or sister. I am convinced, being fully persuaded in the Lord Jesus, that nothing is unclean in itself. But if anyone regards something as unclean, then for that person it is unclean. If your brother or sister is distressed because of what you eat, you are no longer acting in love. Do not by your eating destroy someone for whom Christ died. Therefore do not let what you know is good be spoken of as evil. For the kingdom of God is not a matter of eating and drinking, but of righteousness, peace and joy in the Holy Spirit, because anyone who serves Christ in this way is pleasing to God and receives human approval. (vv. 13–18)

In other words, just thinking about ourselves and our tribe of people is a starting place, not an end. How does our way of living impact others? How does the way we talk, the way we connect, the way we declare standards for living affect people? Does it bring them closer to Christ? Does it produce peace in the people we encounter? Do our lives offer an invitation to joy? Or do we heap burdens and judgment onto others? Is our time spent listening to folks telling us what's right and wrong, and do we feel empowered to accuse and correct others online and in real life?

If someone is distressed over our rules, we are no longer acting in love. All this fighting over eating and drinking, what's clean and unclean, is not the primary goal of gospel living. The kingdom of God is not a matter of eating and drinking but of righteousness, peace, and joy in the Holy Spirit. Anyone who serves Christ this way is "pleasing to God and receives human approval" (v. 17).

―――――

There is a time to stand up and say what's right and what's wrong, but we are to be people of compassion and conviction. What's so challenging about Romans 14 is that Paul is offering freedom to everyone. He's lifting burdens, cutting chains, and focusing us on what matters.

> Let us therefore make every effort to do what leads to peace and to mutual edification. Do not destroy the work of God for the sake of food. All food is clean, but it is wrong for a person to eat anything that causes someone else to stumble. It is better not to eat meat or drink wine or to do anything else that will cause your brother or sister to fall. (vv. 19–21)

What "leads to peace and to mutual edification"?

I want to highlight the word *mutual*, because sometimes I get the impression that Christians enjoy offering edification that encourages other people to believe what they believe, to do what they think is the right thing to do, to vote the way they do, and to think about people the way they do. *Edification* is instruction that helps us improve and grow, but before Paul gets to this, he uses that word *mutual* to push us to evaluate our tendency to think we are always right and that someone who lives and thinks differently from us is always wrong. Mutual edification means that you and I are not always the teacher. We sit with our brothers and sisters to learn. Everyone, even the ones we're judging, has something to offer as people made in the image of God.

> So whatever you believe about these things keep between yourself and God. Blessed is the one who does not condemn himself by what he approves. (v. 22)

Wow, this verse was a kick in the gut for me. I read it and shuddered.

> *Lord, when and how have I condemned myself with what I approve? Help me to not set up a standard over others that is not yours. You are the only One who should be setting standards over others, and your banner over each of us is love. Will you show me how I am resisting the kingdom of righteousness, peace, and joy in the Holy Spirit? Will you convict me of the ways that my life, my desire to be right, my choices, and my words are hindering love and impacting people in ways that drive them away from you? Help me, God, please.*

Pride does not show people Jesus. We don't win people to our side with our fruitless arguments.

God loves the other side.

Heaven is full of people we don't like. Also streets of gold, mansions with foyers, and I hope hummingbird cake. People from Black Lives Matter (the actual organization, not just the movement), immigrants from detention camps, corrections officers, police officers, criminals who got caught and criminals who didn't, children, babies and teens, rich people, people from every nationality on the earth, mean people, evil people, poor people, middle-class people, paycheck-to-paycheck people, nice people, kind people, annoying people, single people and single parents, married and divorced and widowed people, addicts, enemies, and saints. All in the same room together. Together, only because of the King who loved us so radically that, by some thread of grace, we all made it through heaven's gates.

Can you imagine all the missed social cues and faux pas, side-eyes, and pearl clutching that would happen if this group gathered here on the earth? Yes, I can. It's a ruckus few churches are willing to raise, but it is heaven when they do. Love is the resistance. Love creates real change. Because it makes us more like God.

God, who is able to make us stand.

ATTITUDE: God loves me, and no one can take that away from me.

AFFIRMATION: I am capable of loving even my enemy.

REFLECTION: Who do I think does not belong to God or in heaven? Why do I think that?

TECHNIQUE: Work at not being condemned by what I approve. Who am I to declare who and what God loves? Let Love, not approval or condemnation, lead the way.

CONCLUSION

Stubborn Hope

I wish that I could sit with you face-to-face and thank you for giving your time and attention to this book. You are a blessing to me, and I pray I've been a blessing to you. Remember what the good Lord said about those who exercise authority: "Not so with you" (Matt. 20:26). Friend, we are a peculiar people—not the annoying kind—a chosen people who are a wonder to this world. A people who praise because the Lord has brought us out of darkness and into his marvelous light. A royal priesthood utterly besotted with mercy. Our faces shine the love and light of God in dark times because we are a people filled with hope.

The days are difficult. Urgency beats within us as the pain across the earth increases. It is hope that keeps us rising every morning. Hope helps us begin again, reminding us that we are not finished. If we are to remain steadfast in love, we must maintain stubborn hope—the ridiculous audacity to get up again. To try again. To begin again.

Against all odds, we imagine that the world can be different. We believe people can change. We know there will be miracles. We have tasted and seen that the Lord is good. It doesn't matter what the circumstances look like, who is in charge on the earth, or how bleak or hopeless things may seem; we will still lift our arms in worship because the Lord is our deliverer. He is a shield about us. He is our glory and the lifter of our heads. We have a reason to carry on until the end. We will resist the desire to sit down in the muck and stay there. We will carry on with our truth telling, bridge-building, peacemaking, Holy Spirit–filled Bible believing, because we will never give up and never give in. We do no harm, but we take no mess. There is no other path before us.

Let us rise from the ashes by the beauty of hope. Love is our resistance.

DISCUSSION GUIDE

As promised, here's a discussion guide to help you create conversations for change in your book clubs and small groups. Don't forget to message me about your gatherings, if you'd like, so I can pray for you and cheer you on.

Chapter 1: Learning Love

1. Love is resistance. Do you feel the push and pull of love, the unique tensions that we hold in tandem in order to love well? Describe one tension in your life right now.

2. With all the short, quippy sound bites and social media clips that we sometimes reduce faith down to, are you longing for a deeper well?

3. Read 2 Timothy 3:1–5 together. Does this passage resonate as truth for the days we are living in? Why or why not?

4. Share your greatest moment of encouragement from someone you love and respect. Does that tend to inform your perspective, or are you more driven by the

discouragement of those who might have loved you the least?

5. "But we do not get a seat at the table only with the people we love; we sit at the table with the people God loves." How difficult is this for you to internalize?

Chapter 2: Cancel Culture

1. What do you think about the interview at the beginning of this chapter? Do you think these types of conversations are helpful or harmful?

2. When is the last time you saw a conflict, disagreement, or discussion in which there was wisdom, understanding, and humility? (See James 3:13–18.) Why do you think these conversations are rare?

3. Can you believe the Barna study that found young people felt the top three characteristics of believers were: (1) anti-gay, (2) judgmental, and (3) hypocritical? Why or why not?

4. Are there times when cancel culture is actually helpful to hold people accountable for their poor behavior and decisions?

5. Since "cancel culture" is a buzz phrase right now, can you see how canceling happens to people who are not in the public eye more often than we realize?

Chapter 3: Language Matters

1. The Bible is clear that we cannot say whatever we want, whenever we want. How does that differ from our right to freedom of speech?

2. Does our self-proclaimed "Christian worldview" find us acting like Christ—serving people, loving our enemies, journeying with others in a personal, powerful way—or are we found in an echo chamber shouting at or avoiding anyone who does not agree with us?

3. Do we justify using harmful language? If you think so, how have you seen that done? What is the impact on others?

4. If you set your politics aside for a moment, what do you think of the altercation between the two representatives in Congress? What feels frustrating about it? Have you had any similar experiences in your own life? (Remember to be kind and considerate of those in your group who may feel differently from you. When sharing stories, leave out names and keep the share about your personal experience.)

5. How can you learn from people you disagree with?

Chapter 4: Love Thy Neighbor

1. Are you from a community of faith that is hyperfocused on revival or reformation? What do you think about the idea that God is rebuking the body of believers?

2. Do you agree that there is a toxic enmeshment of faith and politics? What does civic engagement look like for a healthy believer and/or community?

3. Have you read Ezekiel 34 before? Does God's rebuke of the body resonate with you? What do you take away from that text?

4. "Selfishness kills connection." Do you agree? How does it kill connection? Do you have an example you'd feel comfortable sharing? (Remember not to use names in

order to respect others and to keep it about your personal experience.)

5. There are no conditions on loving our neighbor (see the story of the Good Samaritan in Luke 10). How did you feel reading the list on the "Love Thy Neighbor" sweatshirt? Where do you struggle most with love?

Chapter 5: Love Is the Resistance

1. Do you think of conflict as a normal part of life? Why or why not?

2. What is your experience with conflict over race, class, gender, or politics? Be careful as you share in a group dynamic, so you can respect other members and their lived experiences. Care for and respect each other as you share. You don't have to agree to discuss.

3. Ashley asked the following questions in chapter 5. Read and reflect honestly together: Do we allow people to evolve, or must they remain in the box we've placed them in? And what does that say about our connections to others? Do we need them to stay where they are to feel good about where we are? Are we tethered to our judgments, or do we let people change for the better?

4. Read Amos 5:22–24 in three or four different translations, then discuss your response to this text. Here is *The Message* version to get you started:

> I can't stand your religious meetings. I'm fed up with your conferences and conventions. I want nothing to do with your religion projects, your pretentious slogans and goals. I'm sick of your fund-raising schemes, your public relations and image making. I've had all I can take of

your noisy ego-music. When was the last time you sang to me? Do you know what I want? I want justice—oceans of it. I want fairness—rivers of it. That's what I want. That's all I want.

5. When you consider the reasons we fight, the conflicts between us, reimagine the world as you know it. If "impossible" is where God starts, then what is the impossible you can imagine?

Chapter 6: When Class, Gender, and Race Collide

1. Do you think we rank each other in society? Why do you think we do this? What's your personal experience with this?

2. "We work backward to move forward. Our past informs our present until we face it, deal with it, and heal it." What do you think about this statement? Is there anything you try to avoid from your past? Is there a next step you can take toward healing this?

3. Is Dr. Helms's White Identity Model helpful for you? Why or why not? Do you consider conversations about race, gender, and class "identity politics," or do you find them helpful for understanding others?

4. "We do have common ground, but when we allow everything to disciple us but Jesus Christ, it feels harder to find." If you take a moment to reflect, what is truly discipling you? What do you spend the majority of your time consuming: news, social media, entertainment, the opinions of others? Or do you keep a healthy rhythm of spending time in the presence of God and in his Word to shape your mind?

5. What does it mean to "Let no debt remain outstanding except the continuing debt to love one another" (Rom. 13:8)?

Chapter 7: Autonomy from Our Camp

1. Do you think the church spends enough time addressing what divides us, offering biblical solutions to our disagreements?

2. In Psalm 51, we see King David moving out of denial about his sin (rape, adultery, murder). Why do you think it usually takes such extreme circumstances for us to step out of denial?

3. Have you considered how race, gender, and religion informed the experience of the woman at the well and her encounter with Jesus? Discuss this together.

4. Sometimes we think that prejudice is brand-new, but it is a tale as old as time. Read the story of Peter in Acts 10 and 11. How did God use a vision to change his heart and mind toward others?

5. We need courage to confront in order to achieve autonomy. What in your past or in your "camp" are you afraid to confront?

Chapter 8: For Lack of Justice There Is Waste

1. What did you think of the Ronald Rolheiser quote about "God hung between two thieves"? Share how it makes you feel to think of the church this way.

2. Do you see a parallel between monoculture farming practices and the more famous side of the evangelical church? Does your experience with Christians tend to be more monoculture or polyculture?

3. There is a painful history between Christians and creation. What examples of this are you personally aware of, and can you share any positive examples of Christians and creation?

4. Proverbs 13:23 says, "Much food is in the fallow ground of the poor, and for lack of justice there is waste" (NKJV). Do you see how the soil a person is born into and grows in can hinder fulfillment of their potential? Why or why not?

5. Read Matthew 20:25–28 and highlight or underline "not so with you." What does this mean for you personally after reading this chapter?

Chapter 9: When Conflict Calls

1. The story of the Mirabal sisters is remarkable. What did you learn from their courage?

2. The conflicts we face are not always imaginable, predictable, or comfortable. What do you do when conflict calls?

3. Minerva's response to the dictator demonstrated she was unshakable in character and resiliency—she was clearly growing the fruit of the Holy Spirit in her daily life. When no one is watching, what are your faithful ordinary practices? Will they sustain you when conflict calls?

4. In conflict, do you tend to respond with fight, flight, or freeze? Why do you think this is true for you? Is there anything else in our list of conflict solutions that felt helpful to you?

5. There seems to be a free-for-all in the digital space when it comes to disagreement. What's your experience

there? How can we grow in healthy conflict, not just in real life but digitally as well?

Chapter 10: Woe to the Offender

1. Forgiveness is a powerful, life-changing experience. It is a healing agent in a world full of conflict, turmoil, and chaos. In the stories that opened this chapter, what do you think of the forgiveness people and communities offered to the killers?
2. Did you know this was the true story of Jonah? What do you think of his reasons for resisting obeying God? Can you better see the merciful heart of God through this tale?
3. "Forgiving the unforgivable takes time for me. It's a process. But I suppose when it comes to necessary, difficult decisions, we make them first and mean them later." Is forgiveness a process for you? Do you have to choose to do it first and mean it later?
4. Do you think Christians perpetually persist in demanding that people calm down in the face of injustice and tragedy? Is there room for anger in our faith practices?
5. "Woe to the offender." Does it bless you to know that the Lord deals with the one who causes the offense, and that he does not just expect the victim to forgive?
6. "There can be no reconciliation without recovery." Do you agree with this statement? How does our resistance to change hinder reconciliation?

Chapter 11: I'll Love You till the Cows Come Home

1. Have you ever had an embarrassing, public conflict? How did that make you feel?

2. Isn't it comforting to know that we need to be both emptied and filled? Can you share a time when you were hungry and the Lord filled you, and when you were rich and the Lord sent you away empty? (See Luke 1:46–55 for reference.)

3. It is difficult to imagine the Lord loving our "tiresome, annoying, disobedient, disedifying fellow Christians," but he does indeed love and welcome them. How does this challenge you?

4. Do you think hurt hinders love? Why or why not?

5. Romans 14 helps us so much in our opinionated culture. How do we condemn others by what we approve? What are some practical ways we can stop this?

A little note from Ashley: I'm so proud of you for starting and finishing this book and doing this work. Sending my love to you and your book club or small group! Kid President says, "Give people high-fives just for getting out of bed. Being a person is hard sometimes."[1] I wish I could high-five all of you. Thank you for allowing me to walk with you as you grow in your love for God and for each other.

ACKNOWLEDGMENTS

Writing a book in a global pandemic while forced to homeschool, moving twice while also pregnant, and then having a newborn with little support and no gatherings in a house where only two of the five family members can wipe their own butts is something else indeed. I'll tell you what I know: the grace of God holds.

To Cody Abercrombie, my lover and friend: you are the reason besides the LORD that I am still saved and sane. Thank you for your support. Our partnership makes it possible for us to work, raise our wonderful babies, and build a life we love (even in lockdown). I love you, and how lucky for you that I finally need that Theragun. To Levi, Lucas, and Willow: I love you with a fierce and abiding love. Life is not easy, but we are with you. May you know the comforting, helpful, and freeing presence of God all the days of your lives.

To my mama: you worked the frontlines of COVID and still found time to be with us. Thank you for all the trips to the beach from New York, and all the sleepovers in California. These pages were possible because of your love for our kids and for me. Thank you for sharing life with us. I love you with all my heart!

To the Abercrombie family, Mamo, Papa Da, Narnie, Uncle Ryan, and Uncle Todd: our time together is rich, and Plainview holds some of our favorite memories. Love you!

To Rick and Macy Grant: we want to be like you when we grow up. Thank you for opening your home, feeding us adult lunchables that went to Harvard, crashing on our couch, and loving our babies. We are so glad to be your neighbors.

To my friends, whose texts, group texts, voice memos, Marco Polos, gifs and direct messages, and (when we could) backyard hangs and socially distanced meals kept me sober and full of hope: Harmony Grillo, Lynette Weaver, Michelle Lutz, Tiffany Bluhm, Saleena Lockett, Katherine Talley, LaTrayl Adams and Katie "Burl" Womble, Ito Aghayere and Leon Hendrix, Gio Adams, Courtney Barry, Jen and Jona Toledo, Kamala Avila-Salmon, Crystal Marie Grant, Chanel Dokun, Jason Walker, Kat Harris, Kait Warman, Cassandra Speer, Shunna and Alex Jones-Moreno, Ryann and Mat Fretschel, Brooke and Brad Wright, Emily Mills, Pricelis Perreaux-Dominguez, Nicki Amoako, Angela Ortiz, Michelle Moore, Tanya Anderson, Zoila LaChapelle, Yessenia Hunter, Andi Andrew, Jo Saxton, and Irene Rollins. Could I be any more blessed with the best humans on the planet?

To the Freedom Road Global Writing Group: oh my goodness, you are the best thing since sliced bread. I wrote this whole dang book with you. Thank you, Lisa Sharon Harper, Marlena Graves, Chante Griffin, and Andre Henry, for starting this and leading us. Special thanks to Deborah, Amy, Anna, Sara, Stephen, Sharon, Grace, and Gigi.

To the Women's Speaker Collective: thank you for holding so many of us steady during a difficult year. Danielle Strickland, Autumn Katz, Susie Gamez, Tiana Spencer, Katie

Castro, Ashlee Eiland, Cheryl Nembhard, Joanna LaFleur . . . I'm thankful such a powerful movement introduced me to so many women I treasure.

To New York City, which kicked my butt for four years straight, and the beautiful Liberty Church Downtown community, where I learned to love my enemy and stay on my knees: thank you. You are forever in my heart!

To Expression 58: thank you for practicing what you preach. It is a joy to do justice, love mercy, walk humbly, and lift my hands in worship with you.

To the Baker Books family: you are my favorites. Rebekah Guzman, thank you for believing in me, sharing your heart with me, and reading my crappy first drafts. Your wisdom is honest and helpful, and I am so lucky to have you in my life! Lindsey Spoolstra, rules be damned, I loved you from jump and may God bless you with extra treasures in heaven for dealing with my comma and citation problems. Wendy Wetzel, thank you for helping me launch two books into the world. I love your heart for people and am grateful to know you!

To the church of Jesus Christ: you're weird, wild, and wonderful. I will never not be thankful for you.

NOTES

Chapter 1 Learning Love

1. "Peggy O'Mara Quotes," Goodreads, accessed March 3, 2021, https://www.goodreads.com/author/quotes/30657.Peggy_O_Mara.

2. "Addiction Statistics," Addiction Center, accessed February 11, 2021, https://www.addictioncenter.com/addiction/addiction-statistics/.

3. Alice Walker, *By the Light of My Father's Smile* (New York: Ballantine Books, 1999), 195.

4. "John 13:34," Bible Hub, accessed February 11, 2021, https://bible hub.com/lexicon/john/13-34.htm; "Strong's Concordance 1781. entello-mai," Bible Hub, accessed February 11, 2021, https://biblehub.com/greek /1781.htm.

5. Rachel Held Evans, *Searching for Sunday: Loving, Leaving and Finding the Church* (Nashville: Thomas Nelson, 2015), 148.

Chapter 2 Cancel Culture

1. Eugene Cho, *Thou Shalt Not Be a Jerk: A Christian's Guide to Engaging Politics* (Colorado Springs: David C. Cook, 2020), 16.

2. Richelle E. Goodrich, *Being Bold: Quotes, Poetry and Motivations for Every Day of the Year* (self-published, 2020), 49.

3. Exodus 35:12; Leviticus 16:12–13.

4. Ephesians 2:14–22.

5. Romans 8:16; 2 Corinthians 1:22; Ephesians 1:14; Hebrews 10:13–15.

6. Anne Lamott, *Traveling Mercies* (New York: Anchor, 2000), 131.

7. Ian Lovett and Andrea Fuller, "Jerry Falwell Jr. May Be Owed $10.5 Million by Liberty University," *The Wall Street Journal*, August 25, 2020, https://www.wsj.com/articles/jerry-falwell-jr-may-be-owed-10-5-million-by-liberty-university-11598395393.

8. Bloomberg, "Megyn Kelly to Leave NBC with $30 Million Payout: NBC News," *Fortune*, January 12, 2019, https://fortune.com/2019/01/12/megyn-kelly-leaves-nbc-exit-terms/.

9. Cameron Knight, "The Washington Post, Nick Sandmann Settle $250 Million Lawsuit Out of Court," *Cincinnati Enquirer*, July 24, 2020, https://www.cincinnati.com/story/news/2020/07/24/washington-post-nick-sandmann-settle-250-million-lawsuit-out-court/5501639002/.

Chapter 3 Language Matters

1. As quoted in Joachim C. Fest, *The Face of the Third Reich: Portraits of the Nazi Leadership* (New York: Da Capo Press, 1999), 90.

2. Kathryn VanArendonk, "Listen to Toni Morrison's Remarkable, Transcendent Nobel Prize Lecture," *Vulture*, August 6, 2019, https://www.vulture.com/2019/08/toni-morrisons-nobel-prize-speech.html.

3. Tommy Beer, "Rep. Ted Yoho's 'Apology' for Cursing at AOC Draws Sharp Criticism," *Forbes*, July 22, 2020, https://www.forbes.com/sites/tommybeer/2020/07/22/rep-ted-yohos-apology-for-cursing-at-aoc-draws-sharp-criticism/?sh=7e7ee15a1b8d.

4. Nicholas Wu, "'I Am Someone's Daughter Too.' Read Rep. Ocasio-Cortez's Full Speech Responding to Rep. Ted Yoho," *USA Today*, July 24, 2020, https://www.usatoday.com/story/news/politics/2020/07/24/aoc-response-ted-yoho-read-text-rep-ocasio-cortezs-speech/5500633002/.

5. Ashley Abercrombie, *Rise of the Truth Teller* (Grand Rapids: Baker, 2019), 22–23.

6. Wu, "'I Am Someone's Daughter Too.'"

Chapter 4 Love Thy Neighbor

1. Robert O' Harrow Jr., "Rallies Ahead of Capitol Riot Were Planned by Established Washington Insiders," *Washington Post*, January 17, 2021, https://www.washingtonpost.com/investigations/capitol-rally-organizers-before-riots/2021/01/16/c5b40250-552d-11eb-a931-5b162d0d033d_story.html; Abigail Abrams and Madeleine Carlisle, "The Republican Party Has Distanced Itself from the Capitol Riot, but Local GOP Officials Fueled Supporters' Rage ahead of Jan. 6," *Time*, January 15, 2021, https://time.com/5930185/republican-party-trump-capitol-mob/.

2. Isaiah 64:6.

3. "Our Best Sellers: Special Edition Love Thy _____: Relaxed Fit Hoodie," The Happy Givers, accessed February 11, 2021, https://thehappy givers.com/collections/this-months-best-sellers/products/special-edition -love-thy-_____-relaxed-fit-hoodie?variant=36832164053148.

Chapter 5 Love Is the Resistance

1. Gina Crosley-Corcoran, "Explaining White Privilege to a Broke White Person," Duke University, accessed March 3, 2021, https://med school.duke.edu/sites/medschool.duke.edu/files/field/attachments/explain ing_white_privilege_to_a_broke_white_person.pdf.

2. Dan White Jr., Twitter post, 6:41 p.m., June 8, 2020, https://twitter .com/danwhitejr/status/1270123820767207425?s=20.

3. Krista Tippett, "Walter Brueggemann: The Prophetic Imagination," *On Being with Krista Tippett*, December 20, 2018, https://onbeing.org /programs/walter-brueggemann-the-prophetic-imagination-dec2018/.

Chapter 6 When Class, Gender, and Race Collide

1. Abercrombie, *Rise of the Truth Teller*, 66.

2. "This Day in History: January 21," *History*, accessed February 11, 2021, https://www.history.com/this-day-in-history/womens-march.

3. @prophiphop, Instagram post, August 27, 2020, https://www.insta gram.com/p/CEZ_hIQgAjD/?igshid=1sz34rb329gk4.

4. Cynthia Silva Parker and Jen Willsea, "Summary of Stages of Racial Identity Development," Interaction Institute for Social Change, accessed February 11, 2021, https://www.sbctc.edu/resources/documents/colleges -staff/programs-services/foc-mentorship/stages-of-racial-identity-develop ment-oct2019.pdf.

5. Kristin Kobes Du Mez, *Jesus and John Wayne: How White Evangelicals Corrupted a Faith and Fractured a Nation* (New York: Liveright, 2020), 169.

6. Nancy Isenberg, *White Trash: The 400-Year Untold Story of Class in America* (New York: Atlantic Books, 2017), 210.

7. Joseph Ferrie, Catherine Massey, and Jonathan Rothbaum, "Do Grandparents and Great-Grandparents Matter? Multigenerational Mobility in the US, 1910–2013," National Bureau of Economic Research, September 2016, https://www.nber.org/papers/w22635.pdf.

8. Ana Swanson, "Striking New Research on Inequality: 'Whatever You Thought, It's Worse,'" *Washington Post*, October 6, 2016, https://www.washingtonpost.com/news/wonk/wp/2016/10/06/striking-new-research-on-inequality-whatever-you-thought-its-worse/.

Chapter 7 Autonomy from Our Camp

1. Ephesians 2:14–18.

2. 2 Samuel 11 and 12.

3. Song of Solomon 1:4–6.

4. Ken Wytsma, *The Myth of Equality: Uncovering the Roots of Injustice and Privilege* (Downers Grove, IL: InterVarsity, 2019).

5. Indigenous Values, "What Is the Doctrine of Discovery?" Doctrine of Discovery, accessed March 3, 2021, https://doctrineofdiscovery.org/what-is-the-doctrine-of-discovery/.

6. "A Deeper Look: The Psychology of Racism (Part 2)," *Al Jazeera America News Daily*, June 27, 2015, http://america.aljazeera.com/watch/shows/live-news/2015/6/a-deeper-look-the-psychology-of-racism-part-2.html.

7. Wytsma, *Myth of Equality*, 45.

8. Idelette McVicker, "Love & Justice: Why Walter Brueggemann's Thoughts Are Stickier Than Organic Peanut Butter," *SheLoves Magazine*, January 27, 2011, https://shelovesmagazine.com/2011/love-justice-why-walter-brueggemanns-thoughts-are-stickier-than-organic-peanut-butter/.

9. Fyodor Dostoevsky, *The Brothers Karamazov* (New York: Farrar, Straus and Giroux, 1990), 44.

10. "Maya Angelou Quotes," Goodreads, accessed March 3, 2021, https://www.goodreads.com/quotes/9821-i-did-then-what-i-knew-how-to-do-now.

Chapter 8 For Lack of Justice There Is Waste

1. Ronald Rolheiser, *The Holy Longing: The Search for a Christian Spirituality* (New York: Image, 2009), 128.

2. "How Chemical Dependence Took Over Agriculture," *Farmer's Footprint*, accessed February 11, 2021, https://farmersfootprint.us/2018/11/16/how-chemical-dependence-took-over-agriculture/.

3. Ray Bradbury, *The Illustrated Man* (New York: Simon & Schuster, 2012), 14.

4. Melissa Denchak, "Flint Water Crisis: Everything You Need to Know," NRDC, November 8, 2018, https://www.nrdc.org/stories/flint -water-crisis-everything-you-need-know.

5. Shawn McKenzie, "A Brief History of Agriculture and Food Production: The Rise of 'Industrial Agriculture,'" Johns Hopkins Bloomberg School of Public Health, accessed February 11, 2021, https:// resources.saylor.org/wwwresources/archived/site/wp-content/uploads /2015/07/ENVS203-7.3.1-ShawnMackenzie-ABriefHistoryOfAgricul tureandFoodProduction-CCBYNCSA.pdf.

6. Brandon Gaille, "47 Interesting Fortune 500 CEO Demographics," *Brandon Gaille*, November 21, 2014, http://brandongaille.com/47-bizarre -fortune-500-ceo-demographics/.

7. Martin Luther King Jr., "Transcript: Interview on 'Meet the Press,' April 17, 1960," The Martin Luther King, Jr. Papers Project, accessed February 11, 2021, http://okra.stanford.edu/transcription/document_images /Vol05Scans/17Apr1960_InterviewonMeetthePress.pdf.

8. Jeffrey M. Jones, "U.S. Church Membership Down Sharply in Past Two Decades," *Gallup*, April 18, 2019, https://news.gallup.com/poll /248837/church-membership-down-sharply-past-two-decades.aspx.

Chapter 9 When Conflict Calls

1. "Rafael Trujillo," *History*, January 29, 2020, https://www.history .com/topics/1960s/rafael-trujillo; "The Mirabal Sisters," *Rejected Princesses*, accessed February 11, 2021, https://www.rejectedprincesses.com /princesses/the-mirabal-sisters; "I shot the cruellest dictator in the Americas," *BBC News*, May 27, 2011,https://www.bbc.com/news/world-latin -america-13560512.

2. Tommy Andres, "Divided Decade: How the Financial Crisis Changed Housing, *Marketplace*, December 17, 2018, https://www.marketplace .org/2018/12/17/what-we-learned-housing/.

3. Colleen Shalby, "The Financial Crisis Hit 10 Years Ago. For Some, It Feels Like Yesterday," *Los Angeles Times*, September 15, 2018, https:// www.latimes.com/business/la-fi-financial-crisis-experiences-20180915 -htmlstory.html.

4. Kathleen Schatzberg, "Hildegard of Bingen," March 2, 2012, Monasteries of the Heart, http://www.monasteriesoftheheart.org/hildegard -bingen-0.

5. James Baldwin, *Remember This House* (n.p.). This unfinished manuscript is the source for Raoul Peck's 2016 documentary, *I Am Not Your Negro*.

6. For a complete list of hotlines for immediate help, please go to https://victimconnect.org/resources/national-hotlines/. Help is a phone call away, and here are four important hotlines you can call right now.

    1. National Domestic Violence Hotline: 1 (800) 799-7233. Available 24/7 via phone and online chat. The National Domestic Violence Hotline is available for anyone experiencing domestic violence, seeking resources or information, or questioning unhealthy aspects of their relationship.

    2. Rape, Abuse, and Incest National Network (RAINN) National Sexual Assault Hotline: 1 (800) 656-4673. Available 24/7 via phone and online chat. RAINN is the nation's largest anti–sexual violence organization. RAINN (rainn.org or rainn.org/es) created and operates the National Sexual Assault Hotline in partnership with more than one thousand local sexual assault service providers across the country and operates the DoD Safe Helpline for the Department of Defense. RAINN also carries out programs to prevent sexual violence, help survivors, and ensure that perpetrators are brought to justice.

    3. ChildHelp National Child Abuse Hotline: 1 (800) 422-4453. Available 24/7 via phone and text. The ChildHelp National Child Abuse Hotline is dedicated to the prevention of child abuse. Serving the US and Canada, the hotline is staffed 24/7 with professional crisis counselors who—through interpreters—provide assistance in over 170 languages. The hotline offers crisis intervention, information, and referrals to thousands of emergency, social service, and support resources. All calls are confidential.

    4. National Suicide Prevention Lifeline: 1 (800) 273-8255. Available 24/7 via phone and online chat. The National Suicide Prevention Lifeline provides free and confidential support for people in distress, prevention and crisis resources for you or your loved ones, and best practices for professionals.

7. Gary Henderson, "How Much Time Does the Average Person Spend on Social Media?" *Digital Marketing Blog*, August 24, 2020, https://www.digitalmarketing.org/blog/how-much-time-does-the-average-person-spend-on-social-media.

Chapter 10 Woe to the Offender

1. Be A King @berniceking, Twitter post, 7:19 p.m., October 2, 2019, https://twitter.com/BerniceKing/status/1179536528026062848.

2. Dietrich Bonhoeffer, *The Cost of Discipleship* (New York: Touchstone, 1995), 45–49.

3. C. S. Lewis, *The Weight of Glory and Other Addresses* (New York: HarperOne, 2001).

4. James 3:1.

Chapter 11 I'll Love You till the Cows Come Home

1. Kathryn Cristaldi, *I'll Love You till the Cows Come Home*, illustrated by Kristyna Litten (New York: HarperCollins, 2018).

2. Rowan Williams, *Meeting God in Paul: Reflections for the Season of Lent* (Philadelphia: Westminster John Knox, 2015), 30–31.

Discussion Guide

1. Kid President, Twitter post, 9:00 a.m., January 10, 2014, https://twitter.com/iamkidpresident/status/421642586198405120.

Ashley Abercrombie is a writer and speaker whose work has been featured in various magazines and digital outlets, including *Darling*, YouVersion, OprahMag.com, *Relevant*, and *Grit and Virtue*. She is the author of *Rise of the Truth Teller* and *Love Is the Resistance*. Ashley is the cohost, alongside Tiffany Bluhm, of the hilarious and helpful podcast *Why Tho*.

For more than fifteen years, she has worked in nonprofit spaces, has led faith-based initiatives, has served as a prison chaplain and pastor, and has spoken at conferences, churches, and events. Ashley has an unrelenting passion for justice, particularly anti–human trafficking and racial justice, and serves as the executive board chair of Treasures, a nonprofit that reaches and supports women in the sex industry and victims of sexual exploitation.

Born and raised in southeastern America, Ashley has called Los Angeles and Manhattan home, so she's got a little Southern, East Coast, West Coast twang. Ashley currently resides in Los Angeles, raising her three kids with her husband and beloved Nespresso machine. Connect with Ashley on Instagram or on her website, where you can read and watch more content about life, justice, and faith: www.ashabercrombie.org.

Connect with
ASHLEY

ASHABERCROMBIE.ORG

Don't miss the hilarious and helpful
podcast *Why Tho*, with Tiffany Bluhm
and Ashley Abercrombie, available
wherever you find your podcasts.

 ashabercrombie  ashleyabercrombienyc

ashabercrombie

TO LIVE WELL,
YOU NEED A LITTLE GRACE AND GUMPTION

If you're tired of smiling on the outside while you are exhausted and lonely on the inside, Ashley Abercrombie has a message for you: it's okay to tell the truth about yourself and get the help you need.

LIKE THIS
BOOK?
Consider sharing it with others!

- Share or mention the book on your social media platforms. Use the hashtag **#LoveIsTheResistance**.

- Write a book review on your favorite retailer site.

- Pick up a copy for friends, family, or anyone who you think would enjoy and be challenged by its message!

- Share this message on Twitter, Facebook, or Instagram:
  I loved #LoveIsTheResistance by @AshAbercrombie @ReadBakerBooks

- Recommend this book for your church, workplace, book club, or class.

- Lead a book club or small group through *Love Is the Resistance*. Download a digital Leader Kit at ashabercrombie.org.

- Follow Baker Books on social media and tell us what you like.

f ReadBakerBooks

🐦 ReadBakerBooks

📷 ReadBakerBooks